Weaving Common Hope

also by **Zach Thomas**

El Fantasma de Gacha
y Más Cuentos de Los Tahkis (2002)

Ghost of Gacha
and More Tales of the Tahkis (2001)

Healing Touch:
The Church's Forgotten Language (1994)

Weaving Common Hope:

A Future for Guatemalan Children

Zach Thomas

Afterword by John Huebsch

ISBN: 1-4107-3175-8 (e-book)
ISBN: 1-4107-3174-X (Paperback)

Library of Congress Control Number: 2003092002

This book is printed on acid free paper.

Printed in the United States of America
Bloomington, IN

Front Cover: Designed by Dave Conlin.
Photograph of Dulce María by Zach
Thomas in Antigua, Guatemala, November, 1997.

1stBooks – rev. 06/20/03

Contents

Acknowledgments

Common Hope's Founder, Dave Huebsch, and his son, John, Executive Director, generously supplied boxes of historical material. Their hospitality at their home in Perham, Minnesota, and at the central office in St. Paul furnished insights essential to the story of Common Hope.

I deeply appreciate the time that staff persons and volunteers gave me in the research phase. My initial request for interviews turned into repeated encroachments on the busy schedules of Kitty Brown (Education Director), Rosa Elena Solís (doctor), Renato Westby (New Hope Village Director), Pat Campbell (Social Work Department Director) and Tamalyn Jackson (Antigua Site Director). The journals kept by Elizabeth McCullough and honorary board member Gerry Carlsen enabled me to take livelier walks with the readers through the villages served by Common Hope. I'm grateful to other past and present volunteers whose responses to my lengthy questionnaire exceeded expectations.

I was fortunate that my wife, Sally, who helped write the project's website, used her knowledge of the project to edit every page and select the photos. For their review of the initial drafts of the book I'm indebted to Dave and John Huebsch, Kitty Brown, Tom and Elizabeth McCullough, Martha Dugan, Sue Patterson, Lynn Miller, Andrea Paret, Wendy Cox, Kathy and George Amble and Cathy Todd. Certainly, their collective memory made this story of Common Hope a more accurate and balanced account. (Names of Guatemalan family members affiliated with Common Hope have been changed in cases where confidentiality was a matter of concern.)

I'm particularly grateful to writers Yvette Nelson and Mary Norton Kratt who contributed their professional editorial expertise for shaping the manuscript.

Thanks to Dave Conlin for contributing his genius at the computer to design the front cover.

I've written this book with regular, ordinary folks in mind, hoping they not only feel the drama of Common Hope but will consider doing something out of the ordinary with their lives. Serving the poor in Guatemala through Common Hope is a great place to start!

Zach Thomas, Volunteer 1997 - 2002
Antigua, Guatemala

Letting Go and Dreaming

Deep purple, white, gold and red bougainvilleas weave flowers and thorns atop high walls one mile south of Antigua, Guatemala. This colorful rainbow marks Common Hope's main site called the Family Development Center. Guatemalans know it as Families of Hope (*Familias de Esperanza*). Once inside the three-acre property, my wife, Sally, and I wandered among gleaming white stucco buildings to locate the main office. Finally, I had to depend on three months of just-completed Spanish lessons to follow directions from a Guatemalan woman. She sent us to the Education Department Director, Kitty Brown. Kitty had served as Common Hope's first on-site manager when Dave Huebsch and his son John (Founder and Executive Director, respectively) moved the project to Antigua in the early 90s. On the day of our visit in September, 1997, the Huebsches were in the home office in St. Paul, Minnesota, so Kitty gave Sally and me a tour of the project.

From Kitty's friendly welcome, I learned that we had graduated from schools across the street from each other in Richmond, Virginia—she from the Presbyterian School of Christian Education and I from Union Theological Seminary. While Kitty had taken her talents to Central America to direct Habitat for Humanity's operations in that region, I had followed paths in health ministries. However, education was the area of service we valued most. Education, as it turned out, was Common Hope's primary reason for being.

Down the corridor, children read books from the project's library. As we passed by, Kitty stopped to explain that the idea of borrowing and returning books was an unfamiliar concept for the thousands of children in the 14 villages served by Common Hope. For that reason they used the books right there on a large table or on floor mats if they needed extra room. Then she patted a child on the shoulder and said, "This is why we're here, to give them the support they need to graduate from school—at least from the sixth grade."

Kitty had been drawn to Common Hope by its multifaceted development work—an approach that avoided making families dependent on the help they received. The Huebsches had found that in working with the poor, education proved to be a key factor in breaking generations of poverty.

Common Hope supports children, their families and the public school system in a manner that increases self-respect and self-determination. The mission sounded practical and workable, but two main obstacles (one financial and the other related to health problems) convinced me that the goal was not easy to attain.

Common Hope addresses the financial problem mainly through a system of child sponsorship, pairing Guatemalan children with families in the United States. In turn, a sponsored child's family automatically becomes eligible for the project's array of services—health care, housing and much more. By this system Common Hope builds incentive into the Guatemalan family to value and

A little boy enjoys a book while sitting in the corridor outside Common Hope's first makeshift library.

support the sponsored child. Obviously, it places a great deal of responsibility on the child, but it's the kind of challenge that the child and family readily understand and gladly accept. Above all, such a family-oriented arrangement makes it financially possible for parents to send a child to school.

On the other hand, health problems create the need for more immediate attention. The Huebsches had learned early on that nothing less than health care available around the clock was adequate to address the physical consequences of poverty—disease, malnutrition and emergencies of all kinds. In the classroom a child with intestinal parasites would not be listening to the teacher.

Along the corridor on the ground floor beneath Kitty's office, a long line of family members affiliated with the project queued to receive medical care. They waited near two small rooms to be attended by a doctor, a medical intern and a nurse. Our brief appearance interrupted their busy workload. Still, the small staff shared generous smiles as their Director, Doctor Rosa Elena Solís, pointed to the new building on the other side of the property that they would eventually occupy. The young medical intern, Edi Rodríguez, proudly informed us that he was one of the first children sponsored by the project—all the way through medical school. I was deeply moved. As we headed toward the new clinic under construction, I kept thinking about Edi and wondering about his story.

We passed between two large buildings that lay parallel to each other—the main offices and a volunteer house. Volunteers come from the U. S. as well as several other countries. Instantly I wished I could be part of that volunteer service community. So did Sally, as I found out when we compared notes later that evening.

The main office building accommodates not only a staff of social workers, but also a warehouse and workteams of a dozen or more people who arrive every two or three weeks from churches, civic groups and other organizations in the U. S. They come in all ages (over 16) and contribute a variety of talents from sorting pills to building houses.

Both Guatemalan employees and foreign volunteers serve as social workers. They monitor the children's relationships with sponsors and assess the total needs of the children and their families. Working together, the social workers, educators and clinic staff coordinate a broad range of services from special education, tutoring and scholarships to dental care, housing, psychological support and much more.

Kitty, Sally and I brushed against walls of wet cement as we wound our way through the clinic building that was under construction. Then we gathered outside in the shade of tall gravilea oaks and stood where an education building would eventually be completed. The project was growing that fast, and I could feel it. Looking back across the property, I surveyed a scene comprised of stonemasons, staff persons, volunteers and Guatemalan children and their families. I've always enjoyed watching new construction underway. However, in this case I was keenly aware that the finished product was going to be more than additional square footage. Rather, the entire effort was geared to building new lives and careers that most Guatemalan children and their families rarely dream about. The project's cultivation of achievable hopes and dreams in the hearts of the poor spoke to our own hearts and called us to participate.

In answering such a call, we were like so many others who, upon visiting Common Hope's projects, want to become part of a solution to the world's glaring problems. We felt a deep desire to do something useful and truly needed by fellow human beings. We knew we had come to a watershed moment in our lives, a moment

Children play together while their parents visit the clinic.

that was as impossible to ignore as the ringing of a bell. It touched our politics, our addictions and our faith.

What we had learned from our church's peace and justice study groups about the history of U. S. foreign policy in Central America made us cringe. Of course, we realized that we were not going to rectify wrongs of the past. Nevertheless, we felt that our integrity was at stake if we merely complained and did nothing.

Mercifully, any possibility of our launching forth purely on the flames of righteous indignation was quickly extinguished. Indeed, our own inner landscapes looked like a flood. We were drowning in too much of everything—too much house, too much work, too much food, too much TV, too much time indoors isolated from life in community, too many activities and too many things. Our biggest need was to have less of everything, except time together. Then again, if anyone had suggested that we exchange 3,000 square feet for 300 in one of the poorest places in the western hemisphere, we might never have left our home. Fortunately, all we had to go on was the need to let go, think small and learn Spanish.

When we began closing down our businesses and looking for someone to rent our house, we felt joyous, like it was definitely the right thing to do. Our Seigle Avenue Presbyterian Church gave us their prayers and blessings one Sunday morning. Ironically, the acceptance of our application at Common Hope connected us with our church in a new way since both the church and the project emphasized education in their work with the poor. When our year's commitment stretched into five years, it was a surprise, but, as I learned later, a very familiar pattern.

At Common Hope we performed a multitude of tasks as they were needed and as we were able. After a year and a half Sally was exhausted from working with a constant schedule of workteams. Moving into a new position as the project's information officer— writing web pages, giving tours and preparing newsletters—was much more fulfilling. Coordinating a Guatemalan women's support group brought her diversity training skills into their ultimate flowering.

After a few months of coping with culture shock, I said yes to a gardening program that John Huebsch wanted to add to Common Hope's sustainable technology services. It took many months to turn a patch of sandy soil into a bio-intensive teaching garden and to train a Guatemalan woman to instruct other women in the basics of home gardening. I worked with John to design the project's own landscape, after which the buying and planting fell under my responsibilities. I couldn't have been happier.

Zach and Sally Thomas relax in Common Hope's flower garden.

Life with Common Hope was mostly outdoors, around simple food and simple pleasures like watching the lava flow down the slopes of volcano Fuego. We laughed often, were close to both

5

children and old folks, generally away from TV and likely at any moment to run into a colorful procession coming down the street. Living in community with 30 people was both challenging and inspiring. Most of all, our efforts had behind them the sense of purpose that comes from work that is truly needed.

We eventually moved back to Charlotte in May, 2002, to be closer to my aging father and to our new grandson. However, our life had changed. It felt lighter living in a different house half the size of our old one. We sold or gave away more than half of our stuff. Finally, we found ways to be useful to an ever-increasing Latino population—something we never would have had the language skills to do before. Back in our home church we expressed our gratitude for these new directions. Sally and I realized that we felt even friendlier to each other.

John Huebsch often says that one of the most important things Common Hope does is to produce changes in the lives of North Americans. "The longest-range improvements in the lives of the poor will come about when the rich see themselves and the poor differently," he tells visiting workteams. Then he adds, "North Americans who think they are poor are in reality rich compared to the poor of Guatemala."

Every day in the project I found confirmation of John's insight. Common Hope brought together Guatemalans and volunteers from around the world for service that had profound repercussions in the hearts of both givers and receivers. The transformation that has occurred in the lives of hundreds of volunteers who have worked with Common Hope is a theme that deserves a separate book. The names of those volunteers are, unfortunately, far too numerous to include here. However, one instance of this weaving together of rich and poor was so dramatic that I interviewed the two families involved to learn more about how Common Hope works. The story takes us back to Edi Rodríguez, the young doctor I had met on our initial tour of the project. He had grown up nearby on the slopes of volcano Agua.

San Juan Del Obispo, Guatemala

Edi was only three and a half years old when he, his baby brother, mother and great-great-grandmother survived the deadliest natural disaster of the twentieth century in North and Central America. It was called "the earthquake of the poor." When it shook the dry ground at 3 a.m. on February 4, 1976, most of the 28,000 people who died were sleeping in houses made of *adobe*, blocks of dried mud.[1] The collapse of these adobe huts released thick clouds of dust, causing death by suffocation. Miraculously, Edi and his family managed to crawl outside and find protection under an orange tree.

Edi barely remembers the event, but his mother, Sylvia, told me that the physical rehabilitation of friends and neighbors made a lasting impression on his life. For months and years afterward, Edi re-enacted with his toys the dramas of medical care that he saw taking place around him. At age 15 Edi nursed his mother back to health after doctors at a local hospital had seriously botched her Caesarian operation. As a result of that experience, Edi swore that he would never again allow a doctor to inflict such poor treatment on his loved ones. He committed himself to doing his best in everything that he undertook and soon found himself at the top of his class, year after year. He dreamed of becoming a doctor.

As I sat with Sylvia under her orange tree, she told me that she never talked with Edi about his dream. "I knew it wasn't possible," she said. "We were so poor that we couldn't help him. Only angels could."

Sylvia brushed tears with the back of her hand. When I looked aside, I saw that a crack still remained in the foundation of their home. Then the congruency in Sylvia's story grabbed me. If "angels" could bring the Rodríguezes safely through an earthquake, surely they could take Edi through medical school.

In 1990, the year Edi graduated from high school, news of his dream came to the attention of Dave Huebsch, Founder of Common Hope.[2] Since Dave believed in promoting self-sufficiency in those he served, he challenged Edi. "Find out what your dream involves," said Dave. "Talk to our project's Clinic Director, Doctor Rosa Elena Solís. She can speak from experience."

What Edi found out was truly discouraging. A scholarship at the University of San Carlos School of Medicine would have to cover tuition, expensive books, medical instruments, "whites" (special uniforms), transportation, living allowance and anything else it took to stay in school for six years. With a long face, Edi reported his findings to Dave.

"I'm going to the United States," Dave responded. "I'll be meeting with people who are involved in our project. I can't promise anything. Let's wait and see what happens."

Avon, Minnesota

Evelyn Budde, along with her husband, Dean, and their four sons had been happily sponsoring several children through Common Hope. She and her family were excited to hear that Dave Huebsch would be making a presentation about the project at their church. Evelyn drove to the meeting alone on that humid July evening.

During the meeting Dave showed videotape featuring Guatemalan children. Evelyn couldn't believe her eyes. She was looking at an interview of six-year-old Sandra López, one the Guatemalan children she and her family were already sponsoring through Common Hope. The videotape, later given to her by Dave, instantly converted her into a puddle of tears. She barely heard another word for the rest of the program. Dave ended his talk with the story about Edi's dream of becoming a doctor. As Evelyn helped him carry equipment to his car, Dave asked her, "Are you interested in Edi?"

"I'd rather sponsor another girl," she answered. "But I'll ask my family."

"Great!" said Dave with a smile as he pulled out of the parking lot.

Evelyn told her husband and four boys about Edi. She added that they could sponsor a girl instead, if they wanted, but encountered unanimous resistance. So Evelyn quickly let Dave know of her family's decision to provide Edi's medical scholarship.

In 1997 Edi graduated from medical school and spent the next year assisting Dr. Rosa Elena at Common Hope's clinic. In 1999 Edi entered the residency program in Radiology at San Juan de Dios Hospital in Guatemala City. With a diploma in hand and a regular paycheck, Edi wrote the Buddes of his abiding appreciation for their help. Even though Edi had never met the Buddes, now he had their blessings and was on his way.

After the financial commitment to Edi was completed, the Buddes focused their energies once again on the other Guatemalan children that they had been sponsoring all along. Then, in early 2000, Dean and Evelyn decided that they would travel to Guatemala to participate in the fifteenth anniversary of

Dr. Edi Rodríguez (a former sponsored child) poses with some of his little patients at Common Hope's medical clinic.

Common Hope and especially to meet Sandra López, now sixteen years old.

Antigua, Guatemala

For the grand occasion of bringing together sponsors and their "godchildren," Common Hope had rented the huge open-air gymnasium of a nearby school. Colorful helium-filled balloons bobbed above tables spread with white paper. Large signs showed Guatemalan families and their U. S. sponsors where to sit together. A dozen tables along the walls bulged with box lunches of fried chicken and soft drinks. The committee planning the anniversary, coordinated by Sally, stationed interpreters at every table.

As the interpreter for the Budde/López table, I waited with Sandra
López and her mother, brothers and sisters. Soon Evelyn and Dean
arrived. At first, the Buddes and Lópezes enjoyed comparing their
differences in skin color, hairstyle and body type. There was so much
hugging that I hardly needed to translate a word. After lunch and
quiet conversation, we cleared the table of chicken bones and french
fries, and the Buddes distributed the gifts that they had brought for
Sandra and her family. The Lópezes were so grateful for the gifts that
they couldn't contain deep feelings welling up. As Guatemalans are
accustomed, the Lópezes delivered long, unrehearsed orations with
many tears. The Buddes listened calmly, gratified for being so
genuinely appreciated.

At the close of the intimate celebration, Evelyn suddenly stood up
and pointed excitedly in the direction of the food tables. "Who is
that?" she asked. "The guy handing out chicken boxes—who is he?"

"That's Edi Rodríguez," I told her. I knew nothing of the
relationship between him and the Buddes. "He's from San Juan Del
Obispo, one of our sponsored children who became a..."

"I know! I know! He's a doctor!" Evelyn said. "We are the ones
who sponsored him! Can...can we meet him? Now?"

"Sure!" I gulped and ran to bring Edi to meet the Buddes.

As the sponsors and the young doctor embraced, I was amazed at
how quickly the roles had changed. Now it was the Guatemalan who
stayed calm while the U. S. family struggled to express deep feelings.
I later wondered who is more vulnerable in the depths of the soul—
the family with economic means or the one with meager resources.
Surely, the question was unanswerable except to say that somehow, in
this case at least, both parties needed each other in an equally
meaningful manner.

Some would say that the Buddes and Edi were likely to meet since
they were already part of larger, underlying patterns.[3] What were the
patterns in this case—receiving and giving, dreaming the impossible
and showing compassion? Are such patterns woven into worlds
hidden in the heart and soul? If so, the encounter in the gymnasium
was not mere coincidence, but a synchronicity—an event that reveals
broader patterns and meanings. Whatever term we use (revelations,

epiphanies, graced moments), such events often provide great joy, the feeling that comes from sensing oneself serving a larger purpose.

The story of Common Hope involves ordinary people who are often pleasantly surprised by meaningful synchronicities. Neither spiritual masters nor experts in development work, project workers learn quickly from mistakes as well as successes, face unknowns with a sense of humor, and practice being patient with the absurd.

If the Huebsch family had lacked these capacities implied in the concept of hope, they would never have ventured to Guatemala—a land in which hope often seems to have been stretched beyond the breaking point between the extremes of rich Latinos and poor farmers. So how and why did the Huebsches come to Guatemala?

That's the question, I must confess, that nagged me for days at the beginning of this writing. I took it to Bill Huebsch (Dave's brother, John's uncle) who has written a dozen books on spiritual and church reform.[4]

I asked him, "If you had to choose the worst period in Guatemala history, when would it be?"

"The 1980s, obviously," Bill answered.

I pressed him for more. "And when you think of a family surrounded by kin and community, friends and farms and all the familiar trappings of American life, who would it be?"

"The Huebsches," he said, laughing at himself.

"Then here's my question. How did the Huebsches, likely subjects for a Norman Rockwell painting, end up in poor thatched-roof huts of Guatemala in the 1980s?"

"Well, if you want a thorough answer you'd have to consult the writings of Charles de Foucault and Carlo Carretto," said Bill. "That's who Dave likes to read."

I recalled these names from my seminary days. They were men who left the safe confines of their familiar cultures in order to go into the poorest lands to do what Jesus taught—namely to help "the least of these." I always smiled at the sheer simplicity of the images that these sources conjured up, and this time I couldn't hide it.

Bill ignored my Presbyterian grin as he waved goodbye and said, "You'll be surprised at the similarities."

11

In the fall of 1984 Dave Huebsch and his wife, Betty, did indeed leave the safety of farm and family in Perham, Minnesota, to begin what became Common Hope in Guatemala. Initially, they chose the towns of San Lucas Tolimán and Santiago on Lake Atitlán. After three years they were confronted on a deserted road between these villages by a band of armed men who told them that they would have to leave the country immediately, or else. Surely at that juncture their plans for serving the poor must have seemed to them about as futile as Edi's dream to become a doctor.

Part One: Early History

Zach Thomas

Ties That Bind

January 24, 1988, San Lucas Tolimán, Guatemala

Betty Huebsch hadn't slept well in two days. Hyper-alert at 5 a.m., she lay fully clothed on top of the bedspread. She heard roosters crowing, rickety carts rattling on their way to market and women in a nearby kitchen pat-pat-patting their corn dough to make tortillas. These were familiar sounds waking the village of San Lucas Tolimán, home for centuries to the Cakchiquel-speaking Maya.

With a slight turn of her head to the window Betty found a breeze to refresh her face. The wind carried its dampness from beautiful Lake Atitlán. The stories she'd heard about the lake's violent birth from volcanic explosions deepened her appreciation of its dependable morning calm. If only she could find a calmness now amidst the violence interrupting her and her husband's mission.

Betty wiped away tears before they reached her pillow, then peered into the dark maze of trusses and rafters supporting sheets of corrugated metal overhead. For months this home had also served as a storage shed for pencils and notebooks for children, clothes and food for needy families, and equipment for so many projects that she couldn't remember them all. Within a day or two they'd have to leave it for good, "or else."

Betty refused to be left numb. She grabbed a pen and notepad to express the thoughts and feelings overwhelming her:

> I feel cheated. It's so unfair that our trying to help poor people has to be halted because someone doesn't agree with our objectives. I guess there's a lot of anger inside me. I feel so desperately helpless for the 1,500 kids who won't be able to continue school, who won't have the teachers we paid, their books, their food program. But we can't risk our lives any longer.

Afterwards, she felt calmer. Maybe she'd be able to sleep in the car on the long stretches of highway through Mexico back to Minnesota. In the pre-dawn pause she revisited the journey that she and Dave had so earnestly begun three-and-a-half years earlier in the fall of 1984.

The empty nest created by their third child leaving for college had presented Dave and Betty with the possibility of doing something together, something different. Conducting retreats for young people had inspired them to consider a life of service to the poor overseas. They had thought about a range of locations from the Far East to South America. One day Dave's brother, Bill, mentioned the San Lucas Mission in Guatemala as a possibility. The idea not only seemed workable in terms of travel, but also the needs were extreme among the Atitecos (the people living around Lake Atitlán). Illiteracy spiked into the 90th percentile, and the infant mortality rate was the worst in the hemisphere. Something about Guatemala called them, and they answered.

The San Lucas Tolimán Mission[5] served 30,000 people through its schools, housing and broad range of health and social services. Fr. Gregory Schaffer had arrived in 1964 to develop a multifaceted ministry to the poor. For twenty years Fr. Greg and his staff of priests and nuns had seen a stream of volunteers come and go, but not many like the Huebsches who fell so deeply in love with the people that they would decide to stay on indefinitely.

Soon after arriving in Guatemala, Dave and Betty heard Ana Vásquez knocking on their door. Wearing her traditional hand-woven clothes, Ana offered a welcoming gift of freshly baked bread. She was a member of the four-hundred-year-old Mission Church, but her husband-to-be, Pedro, was not. She asked Dave and Betty to be Pedro's sponsor so that the couple could have a church wedding. Little did the Huebsches know that Ana and Pedro would become their core of local support.

As Betty lay in the darkness, preparing her heart for leave-taking, she knew she would miss Ana most of all.

Within just a few weeks of their arrival, the Huebsches asked Fr. Greg for permission to renovate the old volunteer quarters. Never mind that the building had been lent to the Guatemalan military to keep them from pestering local folks for free room and board. Never mind that the soldiers had strewn sandbags everywhere, smeared feces on the walls and shot holes in the roof. The new volunteer couple would fix it up.

During the cleaning and repairing, Dave reflected on the Catholic Worker House that his son John had helped develop in Minnesota. He thought it was a good model of working and living in community with the poor. But Dave had also begun developing his own ideas. He wanted a place where volunteers and visitors could live together with Guatemalans. He envisioned a big table where they would work together and laugh during meals. He hoped it would be a place of transformation. The first brochure they produced bore the title "New Visions in Central America" and featured Dave and Betty standing outside this combination emergency shelter and residence. They named the renovated facility House of Hope.

The day finally arrived when they could move into their new home. In last-minute preparations for family visitors from Minnesota, Dave climbed onto the roof to examine repairs to bullet holes. He fell through the roof, landed on a carpenter's horse and broke his back. The first help to arrive was a group of women charismatics who prayed over him. Next came the ox-cart that bounced him along dirt and rock alleys to the local clinic. Finally, Dave had to endure a four-hour ride in the back of a van to a hospital in Guatemala City. The mission driver then dropped Betty at a hotel to wait for Herman, Dave's 86-year-old father, Dave's brother Bill and their son John. As soon as everyone arrived, they re-grouped at Dave's bedside. What a surprise to have a family reunion in the hospital! Dave spent an agonizing week in the hospital while his family visitors went on to San Lucas. He joined them there in a body cast that he would wear for the next four months.

John built a contraption to help his dad in and out of bed. Having planned only a two-week visit that January, John decided to stay through April to help out during his dad's recuperation. He extended his stay for another reason—to learn more about the poverty of the third world. At 23, he was already working with the homeless in the U. S. His experience in Guatemala not only confirmed his calling to serve the poor, but extended that calling abroad. John returned to a job as a mental health specialist at a hospital in Minnesota, but he also promised to lend a hand to his parents' efforts in Guatemala.

Once settled in their new home, the Huebsches' can-do style and broad talents served them well as they began addressing the needs of San Lucas families in crisis. Betty started out working in the mission's nutrition center and cutting hair at the orphanage. Soon she was managing the House of Hope where she and Ana offered hospitality to guests from all over the world as well as Guatemalan families in crisis.

At House of Hope families received a variety of services that helped them put their lives in order. In return, families could "pay" for these services by pitching in with cooking, cleaning and other chores. The Huebsches from the very start required "sweat equity" in exchange for services received, ensuring self-respect in the families.

Wherever Dave looked he saw needs that he could address through his background in teaching and farming. He carried out an irrigation and fertilizer program to improve the per-acre yield of corn. Noting the ever-present scrawny chickens running free, he created a system of fryer chicken production. It was so cost-effective that the Peace Corps adopted it. Several unemployed men found new skills in Dave's carpentry shop called Maya Madera. They made wooden toys for export as well as desks for local schools.

So many needs and so little money eventually led Dave and Betty into an unexpected dead end. They often had to dip into their own meager savings to reach the goals they'd set.

Betty and Dave had a vocabulary for these kinds of experiences. It came from Catholic retreats called Together Encounter Christ (TEC). On "die day," the first day of the weekend events, one faced his or her painful life issues head on. The following two days, "rise day" and "go day," celebrated new growth and renewed energy for service. The pattern drew them closer to the death, resurrection and ministry of Jesus, thus providing a way to take the mystery of their faith into daily life. By the time they left for Guatemala, they'd become leaders in the Minnesota TEC movement and had directed dozens of retreats for more than four years. Their interest in TEC had grown out of the changes they had seen it bring about in the lives of their children. It would not be the last time that they would gain their bearings by paying attention to the younger set.

In the neighboring town of Santiago Dave was meeting with farmers when he noticed that a number of children had gathered. So he put to them the question, "What do you want most in your life?"

"Schools! Schools!" they shouted.

And one of the parents added, "We don't want them to grow up poor like us."

Listening to needs expressed so clearly by the people helped the Huebsches find the focus of their work—improving children's education. Theoretically, this path addressed the core of poverty cycles. Practically, it would mean schools, teachers, notebooks, pencils, desks and much more. Financially, it meant that the Huebsches would become stewards of generous donations from thousands of people they had never met.

By the end of 1985 the entire Huebsch family had settled on the idea of a child sponsorship program—Dave and Betty from Guatemala, John from St. Cloud, MN, Anne from Minneapolis and son Dave home from college on Christmas break. It would give them more control over their work, the necessary financial footing and seemingly endless opportunities for service. Anne designed the logo, two clasped hands in the shape of a heart. The signing of official papers from the Minnesota Secretary of State on January 6, 1986, formed The Godchild Sponsorship Corporation, a tax-exempt, nonprofit, nonsectarian, nonpolitical corporation. Their "Godparent Guide" stated that their basic goal was "...to develop the individual lives of specific children who have been accepted and supported by sponsoring godparents in the 1st world, ...to provide them with adequate education and health care and other basic life needs for long term

Betty and Dave Huebsch enjoy a moment with school children in Santiago.

19

development rather than direct money aid."

In February of 1986 Dave and Betty shared the good news with the villagers of Santiago, and together they began making plans for schools and teachers. Given the distrust that the civil war was causing among Guatemalans, it was nothing short of a miracle that Dave was able to bring together representatives from the National Police, the Military, the Health Department, the Education Department, the Catholic Church and the Mayor and his Council. The attendees applauded the goal of building five schools. They saw courage in the Huebsches, whose work was similar to that of Father Stanley Rother, their former priest. He, like Dave, had come from immigrant German farmers and was also determined to improve the lives of children, half of whom died before age five.[6] Three masked gunmen had assassinated Rother the night of July 28, 1981, in the Catholic Mission of Santiago. The Huebsches inherited Rother's twelve-year-old, four-wheel drive Ford Bronco, and the villagers often mistakenly called Dave, "Padre."

Supported by local authorities, the Huebsches' project grew steadily. The deluge of administrative work poured on John in Minnesota to handle all the correspondence and finances. Photos of children needing sponsors continually arrived. Boxes of wooden toy trucks, colorfully woven bracelets and other handmade crafts piled high waiting to be sold.

A feeling of shared ministry grew out of the personal tone of Dave and Betty's regular newsletters and by the emotionally fulfilling relationships that the project fostered between U. S. and Guatemalan families. The Huebsches' hands-on methods encouraged sponsors to travel to Guatemala to visit their "godchildren." In turn, it also required Betty and Dave to meet a grueling schedule of twenty to thirty speaking engagements every spring and fall back in Minnesota.

By the end of the year, three school construction projects were underway with the first school scheduled to open in January, 1987, in Santiago. In Minnesota John recorded more than 250 sponsors and over $90,000 in total donations for the first year 1986.

The entire Huebsch family spent the Christmas of 1986 together in Guatemala at House of Hope. After personally delivering hundreds of Christmas gifts of blankets and toys, they shared Christmas Eve supper with family and friends like Pedro and Ana (pregnant with their first child). The Huebsch children— John, Anne and Dave—stayed through January to join a team of nine student volunteers from two universities. All worked together to build school desks, pour a cement platform for an irrigation pump and help families harvest corn and beans.

A Christmas gathering in San Lucas Tolimán brings together the Huebsch family. The children are John (standing at left), Anne and Dave (sitting).

Waving goodbye to their children and volunteers, Dave and Betty looked out onto 1987 as though it were a Minnesota landscape, fertile for planting as far as the eye could see. Now Guatemalan children's educational needs shaped the Huebsches' work from both ends. John organized donations of relief items such as clothes, construction materials and school supplies to be shipped to Guatemala. Dave and Betty led school construction in a manner that inspired the people's initiative and participation. Each family in the community agreed to donate a large block of carved volcanic stone every week and provide one person for a day each month to do construction work. Children furnished firewood to cook school lunches by bringing a stick of wood to school every day. Men from local families made desks, chairs and chalkboards while learning valuable carpentry skills. Dave and Betty reported in the spring, '87, newsletter that they had "…managed to get 835 kids into school since Christmas. [They have] hot lunches, notebooks, pencils, and some help with medicine. These poor no longer have a dream in their pocket. They have a prayer God is answering."

During the spring 1987 speaking tour, Betty and Dave told their audiences that because of a change of plans at the San Lucas Mission they would no longer be able to use House of Hope. The situation challenged them to turn distress into determination—a talent they'd come to value among the poor with whom they worked. Instead of flying back to Guatemala, they drove across Mexico in a Dodge van, packed full of more supplies and towing a Jeep Toyota. Anne quit her job indefinitely and hopped in the van to work with them in Guatemala. John stayed to manage the office. Before heading out, Betty told a reporter for the *St. Cloud Visitor*, "We found... a new perspective. Every day we live out a new story."[7]

Dave and Betty confer with some of the fathers who will build schools for their children. The men have already begun cutting stones to be used in school construction.

The new perspective was their dream of a plot of land on which they could build a development center that would house themselves as well as volunteers. They'd even identified the property on Lake Atitlán, but not the necessary funds. In the meantime, Ana and Pedro had managed to find a concrete block building that the Huebsches could afford to rent. It had storage space, too. Good thing, since the shipping container from Minnesota would be arriving soon.

"Maybe all things do work together for good," Betty reminded herself, lying there as the darkness gave way to dawn.

Their loss of the House of Hope heightened their identification with Guatemalans who for years had been living under constant threats to their jobs, land and life itself. At one point in the mid-80s it looked as if the political situation were improving. The bloody scorched-earth counterinsurgency (1982-83) had ended. Vinicio Cerezo, inaugurated in 1986 as the first civilian president in 15 years, pledged to work for the transfer of power to civil authority and even managed to bring the warring parties face-to-face—promising signs.[8]

But Cerezo's tenure soured. He'd made a deal with army officers to ensure their impunity from prosecution for war crimes. Then in the spring of 1987 he encouraged renewed U. S. military involvement in Guatemala. Its Army Engineers began blasting hillsides and bulldozing roads for strategic military access around the periphery of Lake Atitlán.

On their fall 1987 return trip from the U. S., Dave and Betty were not able to get back into San Lucas for several days because of military action in the area. They learned of the increasing number of "disappeared" (*desaparecidos*, a word originating in Guatemala). The number of poor people was also rising—68% of the population below the poverty line in 1987, the largest in Central America.[9]

Dave and Betty's focus was on the poor, not politics. However, the larger military and political forces affected the poor, and that posed a disturbing paradox to Betty's mind. She wrote:

> The people are such great loving people and war seems so unfair. Severe poverty, desperation creeps in and destroys so many people's lives—kids whose fathers are taken, tortured and finally killed…many times right before their eyes. I just can't understand this at all. They are such wonderful people.

Betty and Dave held out alternatives to desperation. At the end of the second year there were 114 new sponsors and increased donations. This financial success funded work in Atitlán that benefited over 1,500 children—three nutrition centers, five schools and dozens of teachers. Maya Madera had accumulated an array of weavings, stationery note cards, liturgical stoles and toy trucks whose sale would help support the work. The chicken project, expanded by funds from Catholic Relief Services, so impressed Guatemalan agriculture officials that they planned to extend the idea to turkey production. The first shipping container arrived in December. However, the festive candles on the Huebsches' Christmas table flickered in a corner of Guatemala growing darker day by day.

In January of 1988 supervisors of the newly-built schools said they'd have to quit. Some of their leaders had been killed, and they and their families had received threats to their lives. Betty and Dave had no trouble believing the educators because things had begun to heat up for them as well. Military personnel detained and searched them more frequently at checkpoints. They learned that their names had begun to appear on lists belonging to death squads. As a result, they stopped taking visitors with them on trips to the work sites and cut their travel in half.

On Friday, January 22, Dave and Betty, as they'd done so often, set out from San Lucas in their jeep. Forty-five minutes later they'd barely entered Santiago when the news greeted them through the car windows that two people had been killed there that morning. Nonetheless, they went about preparing classrooms for the opening of the school year. After a full day of stringing electrical wire, hanging blackboards and washing off desks and chairs, they headed home.

Just outside Santiago, around a curve in front of a sacred Mayan site called Gold Hill, nine men with rifles stopped their car. Neither masked nor uniformed, they were nevertheless well organized and had been waiting for the Huebsches in particular. Dave felt sure they were not an army patrol, but neither did he recognize any of them. While some kept watch on the road, two walked over to the jeep, weapons pointed not from the shoulder but rather casually from the hip. The leader called out Dave's and Betty's names. Instead of a robbery, which at first it appeared to be, the leader told them in a slow, business-like manner, "Your work in Atitlán is interfering with our objectives. You have to leave and never come back." For emphasis he tapped his fingernails on the trigger housing of his rifle.

Then the rest of the group began a lively debate among themselves whether it would be better to kill the Huebsches on the spot. The leader argued that it would be less trouble if they just let the foreigners leave Guatemala on their own. So they let the couple go.

Thankful for a narrow escape from death, Dave and Betty arrived back in San Lucas with grim faces. An hour later they happened to receive a call from John on the community phone. Dave took the call but didn't say a word about the tragic turn of events. (He would wait until he crossed the Mexican border before making a return call to explain what had happened.)

Should they leave for safety's sake or stay and possibly lose their lives? The choice was obvious, yet very difficult to make. Dave and Betty decided that it would be best if the word didn't get out until they were ready to leave. Sitting on a political powder keg, they had to be careful. If families learned that the project was closing, it might light a fuse that could ignite a much bigger problem.

They decided to share the news with the American priests at the San Lucas Mission. The priests needed to be aware of the situation since they could be affected. Dave asked Fr. John Goggin if he would distribute the materials in storage and the second semi-load of supplies that was scheduled to arrive soon. Later that evening and into the night Dave and Betty began packing secretly.

The following day, Saturday, they quietly tied as many loose ends as they could. That evening at supper they shared the news with Ana and Pedro, their trusted friends. They asked them not to tell anyone. It was a scene that kept replaying in Betty's mind:

> I keep seeing everyone around the table as we told them of our leaving. Ana just sobbing with her second child in her arms. Pedro with his head in his hands. Can he support Ana and the children so they don't have to live in a corn stalk hut and dirt floor as they did when we found them? Dear God, please don't let this happen to them. They deserve so much more.

Dave and Betty's daughter, Anne, had left for Guatemala City earlier on Friday. She did not know what had happened until she returned to San Lucas Sunday evening and heard the tragic news. Her decision whether to stay or go was complicated by the fact that she now had a Guatemalan boyfriend.

Monday dawned as a bright and beautiful morning. The project staff filed into work as usual, ready to begin another week. It was a day they would never forget. Upon hearing the news from Dave and Betty, they realized that they could not carry on the work themselves because it would place them in the same danger facing the Huebsches. Dave quickly met with the Maya Madera carpenters, divided the tools among them and urged them not to give in to the temptation of selling their tools to make quick money. Rather, they should use the equipment to build their skills and provide income for their families.

Dave and Betty already knew that they would not be able to talk with the teachers or say goodbye to the hundreds of children in Santiago. That hurt the most. The children were the reason why the Huebsches had worked so hard. Betty closed her writing:

> I feel like we've deserted the children. I don't think Jesus would have left them. So I really cannot follow in Jesus' footsteps. I'm too weak. I truly hope I can be forgiven for this weakness. I sit here so tired. I can hardly write. It's been days since I've been able to really relax and sleep. Will I be strong enough to handle all this and not fall apart? Dear God give me strength.

After many tears and long hugs, Dave and Betty sadly said goodbye to their dear friends, fired up the old blue van and pulled out of San Lucas Tolimán and Santiago Atitlán, on January 25, 1988. On the way to the Mexican border they dropped off Anne with a goodbye hug. She took a bus south to Guatemala City to her boyfriend's house. Dave and Betty headed north, bound for Minnesota.

The week-long trip gave them plenty of time for reflection. What was the identity of the armed men—military, guerrillas, private agents? They could speculate forever. While answers to *what* and *who* remained a mystery, the answer to *why* was certain. The Huebsches had not been handing out Band-Aids. Their projects taught deeper values of self-sufficiency, organizational skills and control of one's life—a rival seat of power, indeed.

Once a group of women had complained to Dave, "Your school is blocking our path to the *pila* (community clothes-washing center)."

Dave replied, "It's not my school. It's yours. You'll have to talk with the men building it."

This put the women in the awkward position of confronting their husbands—totally against Mayan tradition. Yet they spoke to the stonemasons, who quit working on the foundation they'd begun. It would not be difficult to move the footing over a couple of feet. That wasn't the issue. Taking suggestions from women was. Yet they finally did just that. The children got their school, the women their path, and more importantly the community got a taste of the power of personal freedom.

In a letter written later to their supporters, Dave and Betty said that such values "may have seemed like a threat to some subversive groups." The Huebsches were not students of psychological and pedagogical research into the dynamics of development work with the poor. However, their analysis couldn't have been more on target, according to the experts. "The moment [the poor]…struggle for their interests and rights, the regime shows its repressive face," wrote Ignacio Martín-Baró, renowned psychologist from El Salvador.[10] Anyone who helped others think critically or behave independently from the restrictions imposed by terror interfered with the objectives of the oppressors. Both the army and the insurgents had been keeping villages in the Atitlán area under control by unspeakable cruelty. Three townspeople were killed the day the Huebsches left. On their way out, a priest told them, "You're lucky to be alive."

The Huebsch homecoming was bittersweet. "Welcome back Dave and Betty" read a big banner at their St. Lawrence Catholic Church where friends gathered around them to give thanks for a safe return. The warm welcome soon gave way to the cold and snow of February in Minnesota.

After settling back into their home, the first task was to let the donors know what had happened. Dave and Betty sent out a letter explaining why the project was forced to close and encouraging donors to extend their generosity to other worthy groups. John closed the office and drove home with a carload of boxes and files. He understood well his parents' grief over leaving Guatemala. It was a loss for him, too. Before leaving, he put his arm around his mom and said with his characteristic good humor, "I'll continue to file zeroes on the project's tax return. So the project still legally exists, you know—just in case we change our minds."

By spring Dave and Betty saw that the winter wheat they had sown prior to leaving in 1984 was now being replaced by weeds growing up through the bailer, combine, corn picker, mower and cultivator they had left in the field. Repairing what could be fixed, mending fences and chopping wood proved therapeutic for letting go of the disappointment.

Betty somehow knew she would return to Guatemala. She intuitively understood that the universe ran on a kind of emotional logic—the deeper the pain, the greater the possibilities. Betty was no stranger to pain. Mark, her firstborn, was only two when he died in an accident. Cheryl, her fourth, died at only six years of age from a two-year struggle with cancer. The rest of her children left home to lead their own lives. Now, terror separated her from 1,500 Guatemalan children for whom she felt responsible. Wherever she had lived, Betty's home was always full of family, friends and even strangers in need. To be living now in an empty, quiet house felt odd, indeed.

Possibility danced into view later that spring when Anne called from Guatemala. She was married and pregnant, a great excuse for grandparents-to-be to drive down for a visit. In June of 1988 Dave and Betty drove back to Guatemala to see Anne. They also visited Ana and Pedro in Atitlán. Aching to return to their work, the Huebsches discreetly investigated that very possibility, but found it was still not safe. However, they did find some developments in San Lucas and Santiago that encouraged them. Children continued to attend the five main schools they'd begun around Santiago. As planned, the schools had been converted to the national system, so that now the government paid for each school's director. Among the several other schools they'd supported, only one had had to close. The vocational school for welding and carpentry had divided into three workshops, each with its own crew.

Back in Minnesota Dave resumed his English teaching job at the local high school and inaugurated the Spanish classes there. He and Betty offered one-day retreats to parishes and other groups on spirituality, discipleship and service. However, whenever they discussed what lay ahead for them in the years ahead, one question kept coming up. Was there a future connecting them to Guatemalan children? The issue burned like an eternal flame.

Over breakfast on the last day of school before Christmas 1989, Betty and Dave made a final decision to take up the project again. Betty spent the day savoring their decision to return to serve the poor.

It felt good. After supper she developed one of her migraine headaches—one so severe that she asked Dave to take her to the emergency room. What should have been a routine trip became a different kind of journey for Betty. She died unexpectedly from a blood clot lodged in her brain. It was December 22, 1989. She was 53 years old.

Betty's grave stone contains two important symbols of her earthly pilgrimage—a piece of granite in the shape of Guatemala and an engraving of two clasped hands in the shape of a heart.

Father-Son Team

In his grief Dave found things to be grateful for. The spring thaw announced the opening of fishing season in Minnesota. From his deck overlooking the Ottertail River he watched John on the bank casting a daredevil lure for whatever would bite. The scene lifted Dave's spirits.

The gratitude welling in Dave came primarily from reflecting on Betty's life. He was glad that he and Betty hadn't waited for a "better time" to venture out together. "Look at the gifts God had given us that otherwise we would never have discovered and put to use," he told family and friends. He'd been pleasantly surprised to learn how easily Betty adjusted to living as simply as they'd had to live in Guatemala. Wherever Betty went she was always at home. Hospitality was her gift. She provided room, food and a welcome that drew people into friendly space. Dave remembered Betty's gift of freely giving that bore such fruit in Guatemala. She gave away practically all she had—so lucky, he thought, to have done so before she died. No one could have been better prepared to go.

Dave saw Betty's nature continuing to flow through John. He, too, had gifts for service to others and was content to live modestly. Maybe the project had not come to a dead end. Maybe like the river, or like the energy of the next generation, the project still moved on. Dave made his way down the bank and brought up the subject with John.

Even as a 29-year-old, John got a kick out of listening to his father's unending flow of ideas. In this case, the main thing John wanted to know was whether going back to Central America was an obsession or something they would be doing of their own free will. His dad convinced him that the choice to re-start the project would be just as real as the choice they'd already made to put it down and walk away. They both had plenty else they could do.

John was impressed by his dad's ability to leave something behind and take up the new. His earliest memory was of being carried face down from their house as it was threatened by the barn burning nearby. Everything—farm animals, machines, cars, and tools—went up in smoke. Next day, before February turned the melted earth back to concrete-hard ice, Dave hired a bulldozer to bury the entire rubble in a giant hole.

"You can't always control life's changes, but you can choose the next step," said Dave.

John knew his dad would say this. He just needed to hear him say it again. It was one of those traits he respected most in his father and hoped he could replicate in his own life. John also wanted to make a healthy transition. Leaving his mental health job and divorce mediation practice was the easy part.

Only a personal issue remained—his girl friend. Was there a future in that relationship? He sensed it had come to a standstill. Going to Guatemala would push it one way or the other. He prepared to give it up, set the relationship free and trust that the outcome would be for the best. The calling to Guatemala was immediate and real. That would come first.

John plopped his lure between two dead branches right beside a log jutting from tall grass. "That deserves one," he said.

Dave thought so, too—a perfect toss. He felt genuine respect for his son's talents. It pleased Dave that so often he and John complemented each other—he, Dave, the inventor and teacher and John, the developer who could jump on a good idea and make it work.

John and Dave Huebsch pause during one of their many informal conferences.

John yanked his rod and reel and brought the prize onto the dock. "Nice bass!" he and his dad said in unison. And without one word more, they both knew that they would be returning to Guatemala together.

Before the spring of 1990 had finished decorating the woods and meadows around Perham, MN, Dave and John were already preparing to start up the project once again. Neither of them felt a need to broach the matter of whether their father-son team would actually work. Why should they question it? For almost

31

three years John and his parents had managed the project in Atitlán successfully. They had learned along the way how (and how not) to run a project. With Dave and Betty in Guatemala and John in Minnesota, the relationships had been well defined by distance as well as by separate areas of responsibility. The new venture, however, would require them to work closely together and to do some serious soul searching regarding their respective roles.

In June of 1990 John and Dave flew to Guatemala City. Anne's house and pick-up truck served as a support system for scouting out a new location. Dave and John still carried with them the dream of a few acres on which to build a center, but this father-son team acted on wiser priorities. Listening to the people's desires came first. Before they could even think of construction, they would have to find where their skills and interests best matched the needs of the people—a process of listening to the people and trusting intuition mixed with experience. As Jesus said, if you followed him among the poor, it would be much like fishing. Dave and John could relate to that.

Unable to return to Lake Atitlán, they set out in new directions. Looking for a place of deep poverty, they hoped to avoid the strife of armed conflict, especially since they intended to invite the help of volunteers. In Nicaragua a cease-fire agreement had just been signed in April between the U.S.-backed *contra* revolutionaries and the Sandinista government. In Managua and Jinotega they interviewed educators, lawyers, municipal and health officials. The need for technical assistance in Nicaragua was great, but their hearts pulled them back to Guatemala.

While in Guatemala City they went to the Military Geographical Society to ask for a map of the Atitlán area. A soldier checked to see if the Huebsch name appeared on any of their records. Then, the captain said as he handed over the map, "It's coded. If we find it in the wrong hands, we'll know where they got it." Dave and John knew that if their names had been on a death list, the military would not have provided the map. So they breathed more easily not having to worry so much about the Guatemalan army.

In Antigua, Guatemala, they looked for a project called Belén. Finally, they happened to run into a Belén social worker on the street, and she led them to the project. There the Huebsches met the clinic doctor, 27-year-old Rosa Elena Solís, a recent graduate of Guatemala's San Carlos Medical School. Rosa Elena specialized in pediatric medicine and planned to return to the Social Security Pediatric Department in Guatemala City where she had begun her career. She agreed to accompany John and Dave to villages on the outskirts of town where a number of her patients lived. She was sure that they would find many families eager to form relationships between U. S. sponsors and their children.

Antigua, population 30,000, sits like a postage stamp on a 30-square-mile ancient lakebed, elevated to over 5,000 feet. Three towering volcanoes compose the southern and western horizons. To approach the village of Hermano Pedro, John, Dave and Rosa Elena drove from the elegance of Antigua to steep escarpments along the town's northern and eastern rims. They made their way up a narrow dirt road that also served as a drainage ditch during rainy season, May to October. Initially, they saw families that were fortunate to be living along the road. Their lots measured only 25 feet wide and less than 50 feet deep before heading at impossibly steep angles almost straight up. "Up" was where the not-so-lucky lived.

On foot they crossed a stream at the community *pila* (clothes-washing basin) and then held onto saplings to pull themselves along switch-back foot trails. Every few yards an opening in the vegetation allowed a view below onto a roof of metal or plastic material and an adjoining 40-80 square-foot clearing that served as combination play area, kitchen and storage space. In a corner, black plastic nylon curtained off a latrine. Having literally carved these lots into the hillside, families retained the sandy earth by carefully locating sections of discarded chicken wire, tree trunks, bedsprings, and a variety of automotive parts. Stalks of sturdy yucca also protected against erosion and neighborhood dogs. A 10' x 20' shack of cardboard, plastic sheeting, corrugated metal, end pieces of lumber, tree limbs and car doors might be housing as many as eight to ten people. In heavy rain even the cleverest network of ditches could not prevent streams from taking short-cuts across the dirt floor. It was not uncommon for a merciless downpour to carry entire dwellings downhill.

John and Dave looked into the trusting brown faces and dark eyes of the children. Having confidence in Rosa Elena, the mothers held up their babies so that the foreigners might give a customary blessing in the form of a touch on the head. Who were these poor people whose souls shone so brightly through their smiles, who craved attention and who were so willing to be photographed?

The families were a mixture of Mayan and Spanish populations. In one out of every five households the father had abandoned the family. Half of the fathers who could be accounted for had problems with alcohol. The income of the families was around $100 a month but varied greatly depending on the occasional or seasonal work available. The families had an average of four to five children living past age five, and in all likelihood had nearly that many more who had died from malnutrition or dehydration before then. Basically living without health care, adults on average died in their sixties (men some six years earlier than women). One of every three adults could not read or write, and only half the families owned the land on which they lived.[11]

The children of Filiberto and Elena Salazar demonstrate that, even in the most humble homes, children may find love and support.

Were there other places in Central America that the Huebsches might have visited where the poverty was even more severe? Apparently not, according to researcher Tom Barry. Guatemala has "...the highest infant and child mortality rates, the lowest life expectancy, the most malnourished population, ...the lowest level of public health expenditures...[and] the least-educated society in Central America."[12] How could this have happened? The answers reside in ancient historical structures and ongoing economic factors.

In reality, Dave and John were looking at the descendants of Guatemala's 22 indigenous Mayan groups. They had a long history of oppression beginning in the early 1500s with their defeat at the hands of Spanish conquistador, Pedro de Alvarado. Not much had changed since then. Antigua, founded in 1541, served as the capital for 230 years. The governing officials distributed large tracts of land to military, political and religious authorities. These royal grants included the right to use the inhabitants as serfs who would work the land. The landowners' policy of choosing peasants to collect taxes from their own people created a bureaucratic class that buffered the elite from the lower classes.[13] Such hierarchical structures, reinforced by the burgeoning coffee industry beginning in the late 1800s, remain in place today with only a few modifications. As a result approximately three hundred families, less than two percent of the population, control more than 65 percent of the land worth farming.[14] The vast majority, therefore, have to take jobs that perpetuate the hierarchy.

In modern times, the sad conditions caused by this antiquated social arrangement are being made worse by economic factors and a steadily increasing population. Economist John D. Abell reports that after two decades of tutelage under the International Monetary Fund and World Bank, Guatemala's Gross Domestic Product per capita "…in 1998 [was] actually less than it was before the country signed on to the banks' programs…."[15] Ross and Gloria Kinsler, long-term Presbyterian missionaries in Guatemala and Costa Rica, report that the late twentieth century shift away from human development and towards an obsessive concern for accumulation of wealth was making "…the rich richer and the poor poorer."[16]

These are the historical and economic conditions that left behind the conquered, the dispossessed and the victims of increasing inequality. Two tall Minnesotans peered into those brown faces and saw something of Jesus. Turning to each other, Dave and John said, "Yes! This is the place!"

As the number of photos grew, the Huebsches looked for someone to write down the names correctly and keep records. Rosa Elena took them out again, this time to the house of José Adolfo Monroy Pichiya. He'd just terminated his work as a small business advisor after three years with the Belén project. Adolfo answered the knock on the door.

With assurances from Rosa Elena, he went directly with them to explore the other villages south of Antigua.

In San Juan children feared having their pictures taken as long as there were soldiers in town. John, Rosa Elena and Adolfo recommended leaving, but Dave walked over to the mayor's office and asked him to ring the church bells. The mayor did just that, the soldiers disappeared, and the children came running out. Mayra, severely deformed by spinal meningitis, was carried by her mother, who told Dave she didn't think anyone would want to sponsor such a child. Dave said she was wrong because he would be the child's sponsor himself. Learning that the mother spent hours every day pulverizing food that Mayra could swallow, Dave later bought her a blender.

Before leaving the country Dave told Rosa Elena and Adolfo that he and John would be back in the fall and wanted to employ both of them in the new project. The two Guatemalans welcomed this good news since they expected the Belén project to close by year's end.

On the airplane home, father and son looked at their catch—photos of 160 children, each one precious. Before the end of the year they would find sponsors for nearly every one. Now the children could anticipate not only mail and gifts from "godparents," but also futures beyond pipe dreams and hopes beyond cycles of despair.

By November, 1990, Barb Hansen, a colleague of John's on the Mental Health Unit, had converted her basement into Common Hope's home office. She would serve as the office manager. Now all that stood between the Huebsches and Guatemala was the week-long trip through Mexico—again, blue van pulling red jeep. If Dave and John needed a sign from heaven to assure them, they found one south of Mexico City on the side of the road right where the van's electrical system, regulator and battery died. It read "Electricity For Cars." In a couple of hours the sign's owner had fixed the van with spare parts from his junkyard.

South of Antigua in San Pedro El Alto, Dave found a hospitable family with enough space for a little office in addition to sleeping quarters and super-cold showers. John attended Spanish classes nearby for five weeks while Dave picked up Adolfo in Antigua every day and gave him a lift to the San Pedro office.

Adolfo Monroy helps children and their parents write and decorate Christmas thank-you letters to Common Hope donors.

Adolfo, in his mid-twenties, was the first official employee. He called himself the "office manager." The second of four sons, Adolfo lived in the neighboring town of San Cristóbal and was studying for a career in law. Dave loaded him with camera and video equipment to photograph children. Then he taught Adolfo how he wanted the information organized.

With Christmas approaching, Dave, John and Adolfo realized they'd have to hustle if they were going to give out Christmas baskets to the 150 affiliated families. By late Christmas evening the Huebsches and all of Santa's helpers had delivered baskets to many happy families. Two days after Christmas the crew looked at one another and realized they had not prepared a single holiday thing for themselves. Or had they? In the December newsletter John and Dave shared that, "It was good to be able to forget about ourselves long enough to experience the best Christmas ever."

A timely gift, however, did arrive through a family studying with John at the Spanish school. They told him that the house they were renting on Ninth Street in Antigua would soon be vacant. It had two levels, a small courtyard and, yes, hot showers. John made a deal with the owners and by mid-January, 1991, the house, which would serve as both home and office had been totally outfitted. They disassembled old crates to make shelves, transformed a nook into a dark room, restrung wire for the computers and hung a sign outside that read "Children of God Project."

Once in Antigua, John knocked on the door of Curt and Sally Jackson, missionaries who for three years had been helping children whose parents worked in the market. The oldest of their five children, 14-year-old Tamalyn, answered the door. If Dave and John had known that they were looking at the future director of the Antigua project, they wouldn't have believed it. Then again, they might have. After all, they were in the business of creating futures. Eight more years and Tamalyn would graduate from a U. S. college with a degree in international relations. Tamalyn's hidden talents were already being woven into future patterns.

Dave had hoped that his friends, Ana and Pedro from San Lucas, would join them in the new work at Antigua. They finally agreed, and with their arrival in March, Ana took the cooking responsibilities off Dave's and John's hands. Pedro put his photography skills to use once again.

There was now a core team of eight staff, plus one volunteer who helped women start up small businesses such as juice shops and plant nurseries. News of the project's presence traveled quickly through the villages by word of mouth, ensuring that the team's increased capacity would attract greater numbers of needy families.

Adolfo's knowledge of legal matters and local customs provided a valuable reference for making wise decisions. He knew that bringing electricity or water to a family could not be done simply by stringing wire or laying pipe. It required walking the requests through a variety of neighborhood and village authorities.

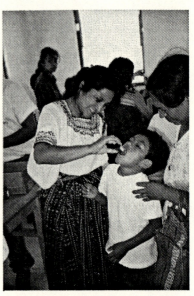

Ana Vásquez gives medicine to a child to help prevent parasites.

Providing food or school supplies would also be impossible without some way to remember the families and the kinds of services each was receiving. Dave developed a computer program he called *Niños* (Children) and taught Adolfo and the other staff how to use it. Now every child had his or her story kept safely in the project's computer memory.

Getting to know the children and their families proved easy in comparison with developing effective responses to their needs. The core team found that the challenges of helping needy families tended to make social workers out of them all. Everyone did everything. Even office workers hammered nails for a family's new home. Whoever was closest to the phone answered it. Whoever was

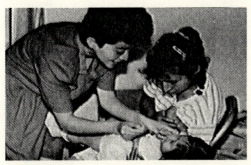

available in an emergency drove the patient to the hospital. Fortunately, the Belén facility had not closed as expected, so children could be referred there to see Rosa Elena. In the meantime, commonly used medicines were dispensed from a room in the Antigua office. This little pharmacy would take a few more years

Dr. Rosa Elena Solis cares for a sick child brought by her mother to Common Hope's medical clinic.

to grow shelf by shelf into the project's clinic.

The shoulder-to-shoulder effort created tight bonds among the original project workers who even now recall those days with nostalgia. However, it was also exhausting work. At times no one wanted to answer the phone for fear of having to respond to one more medical emergency.

John felt that the project's medical services in particular could respond more effectively to the constant demands if they were better organized. After talking it through with Dave, John decided to create a separate project to address medical needs specifically. Beginning in June of 1991 after fundraising presentations in Minnesota, John stayed at home to organize the complementary project. This gave him time and space to clarify his role in the scheme of things. The move afforded Dave the same opportunity.

Though Dave was now the only Huebsch in Guatemala, he fortunately had plenty of assistance. In the fall of 1991 the first waves of long-term volunteers from Minnesota began to arrive, eager to be of service. The crowd of extra helpers at the Ninth Street facility plus the growing demands from poor families made the idea of a center for services and volunteers less of a dream and more of a necessity. The number of sick and homeless who were showing up began to outpace the project's capacity to respond. It was characteristic of Dave to go the extra mile, and increasingly he had to do so, as with René, a young hemophiliac boy.

Suddenly one evening René appeared at the door with a hemorrhage. Dave rushed him to a children's hospital in Guatemala City only to find that they had no matching blood type for René. Driving all over town in the night rain, Dave finally located a doctor who opened his clinic. Returning to the hospital, Dave saw that René was so weak that he couldn't even hold the little toy that his sponsors had sent. The staff was amazed that Dave had been able to find exactly what they needed—blood of the correct type in plastic bags packed in ice. Dave's extra miles had saved René from the immediate life-threatening emergency, though his long-term prognosis remained in doubt.

Beginning in his 1992 newsletters, Dave began to write more openly about his feelings. Experiences like René's, day after day, took their toll. "I wish I would feel less of the affliction that poverty brings," he told his constituents. The emotional strain intensified. It caused him to think of his friends and family back at his home parish. "They all seem so far away. I sense the great distance and separation exacted by my work here," he wrote.

Dave was experiencing the range of emotions that "faithing it" brought—not only his faith, but also the faith of the poor that seemed to come from nowhere. Hearing René's family praying so earnestly for his recovery, filling a request for a sewing machine from a man missing a leg and an arm so he could provide for his family, "one cannot experience such events and not be changed," Dave reported.

In truth, the change was more like a calling and, apparently, had been growing louder for decades. Dave had served on the parish council at his home church, had taught religion classes to high school students and had always been known as one to whom youth turned for counsel. Now without the comfort of Betty or John at his side, he was leaning more closely on his spiritual resources and seeing more clearly how a higher power was using his life to bear fruit in desolate places. Finally, he concluded, "I have to learn more about this Jesus I have met."

In the spring of 1992 Dave called John to tell him that he had been thinking seriously of entering seminary, a four-year commitment. He wanted to discuss the possible effects his decision might have on the work they had begun together. It was not an easy call to make. Afterwards, Dave walked down to the San Francisco Church to light a candle for René. René's eventual recovery was a time of celebration for both René's family and for Dave. Perhaps unconsciously, Dave had also lit the candle to shed more light on his own path and that of Common Hope as well.

Zach Thomas

Part Two: Organization and Programs

Zach Thomas

We're All In This Together

Dave made it clear to John that he would not go to seminary in the fall of 1992 if it meant closing down the Antigua project. John agreed to take over as Director so that his father could follow his calling. However, this meant that John now had two organizations to think about—the one already in progress led by Dave in Antigua and the new health related project that he, John, was creating also from a base in Minnesota and also destined for Guatemala. John and Dave realized that the turn of events could prove confusing to donors, especially since Common Hope had already launched a capital campaign to construct the "Project Center and Health Care Facility" in Antigua. Adding pressure to the cooker was the fact that they had not yet found land on which to build. As they considered merging the two boards of directors, John called Kitty Brown to see whether she would be interested in living onsite in Antigua and managing the combined operation.

Kitty and John had been in touch over the past year. Kitty had worked extensively in Central America for seven years with Habitat for Humanity and knew Guatemala well. But she also knew herself, burned out from work south of the border and generally not interested in child sponsorship programs. All she wanted was to settle in the U.S., find a nurturing faith community and adopt a child. She was on her way toward these goals, having just rented an apartment and having found a new job in the mountains of North Carolina. Had she not already planned to visit her sister in Madison, Wisconsin, at the end of May that year, she might never have agreed to drive seven hours farther west to meet Dave and John in St. Paul.

When she arrived, both John and Dave were very distressed. They had just gotten word that Pedro, Ana's husband, had been killed in a car accident near Guatemala City. After supper it was a somber trio that headed out to the board meeting.

By prior agreement with Dave, John presented a plan to expand and restructure the project toward the broad-based goal of community development. Kitty had to admit as she left the meeting that she was impressed with the integrity of the organization and its vision.

What the revitalized Huebsch philosophy proposed was as important as what it eschewed. The Huebsches had no interest in becoming political activists or religious crusaders. They made it clear that they were putting their Christian faith to work, but not as a requirement either for those they served or for those who joined in the volunteer effort. They would describe themselves in this manner: "[We are] a Christian organization, yet [one that] is non-denominational and serves the poor without regard to their religious affiliation. [We] encourage Christian ethics and spiritual development on a personal level [and] seek to carry out the mandates of the Gospel in a peaceful and non-forceful manner."[17] Their guidelines grew out of their focus on the child. Their commitment was to:

- Serve the poorest children and the families who support them.
- Preserve human dignity and life.
- Strive to be culturally sensitive in our planning.
- Create life support systems where they do not exist.
- Improve living conditions whenever possible.
- Provide opportunities for volunteers to share their gifts and talents.
- Prevent life-threatening situations, while being prepared to respond to emergencies.
- Encourage systematic change by sharing information.
- Empower people by teaching independence.
- Do only that which people cannot do for themselves.
- Work peacefully to raise public awareness of injustice.
- Use our resources wisely and efficiently.[18]

This model definitely caught Kitty's attention. She knew from previous experience that whole families and communities have to be involved if the children's education is to succeed.

"Do you want to join us?" the Huebsches wanted to know.

"I have a new job, new apartment and a wedding to attend in Boston in September," Kitty said.

"No problem," said John. "If you can be in Guatemala by July, that'll give you two months training with my dad before he goes to seminary in September. Then you could return to the U. S. and attend the wedding. While you're back in the states, think about us, and we'll be thinking about you. If we both agree, you'll be the new Site Director in Guatemala."

Arriving in Antigua on July 2, 1992, Kitty paid little attention to the cramped Ninth Street quarters in Antigua. Her focus was on learning everything Dave had time to teach her about computers, photography dark rooms, newsletters, construction and more—most of which was already part of Kitty's broad work experience. They worked 14- to 16-hour days together. Kitty was very impressed with Dave's expertise in so many areas and with the project's overall commitment to an integrated development concept.

Kitty Brown poses with a young man who has received a bicycle as a gift from his sponsors. They will receive a copy of the photo and a thank you note from him.

Back in Boston at the wedding and wherever she went, Kitty shared the brochures and photos of the project. The more she talked about it, the more she realized that she truly was committed to helping it grow. The contract between her and the Huebsches was sealed with a phone call, and Kitty arrived back in Antigua on October 1, 1992.

Kitty took over Dave's old office and woke up the next morning to begin facing the stark realities of education in Guatemala. In the early 1990s almost half the children from 7 to 14 years of age did not attend school. Fewer than 20 percent of those who attended school managed to finish the sixth grade. Only 16 percent registered for junior high school and one percent for high school.[19] The latter had only a handful of career paths from which to choose—secretary, teacher, accountant or tour guide.[20] Even though at the end of the decade of the 90s these statistics would improve a little, Guatemala's educational record would still rank it near the bottom of Latin American countries, ahead of only Haiti.[21]

Making matters worse, the scant education that Guatemala provided[22] hardly nurtured the skills necessary to create a life different from the past. It focused on rote learning and memorization, overlooking the development of a critical awareness of history, knowledgeable participation in the society and creative re-visioning of the future. To follow these latter paths required a profound trust in the creativity of the students. In Guatemala, where fear rather than trust abounded, educators found it more convenient to treat students as receptacles of information. This "banking" model considered education as a deposit to be made, not a process to be nurtured.[23] It controlled all the "input" and "outcomes" that served the status quo. In summary, without intellectual growth, the children lacked precisely what they needed to build a better future. Without quality education, the only guarantee children had was the familiar cycle of poverty.

The specific objective of Common Hope—to help a child finish at least the sixth grade—seemed right on target, the exact point at which to make the biggest and longest-lasting inroads on poverty. It also seemed like a modest ideal. So why would this goal require such a broad family and community development approach as the Huebsches were planning? Why in ten years would the project need a center, twenty-five long-term volunteers and a Guatemalan staff of almost one hundred? One needs only to look at the financial condition of the average family that the project began serving in the early 90s.

A typical family in one of the sixteen villages south and east of Antigua is very likely deeply in debt at the end of the year since most of its average monthly income of $100 to $150 comes from seasonal work on a coffee plantation earlier in the year. Harvesting coffee takes place during January through March, and the school year runs from January to October. Therefore, the main opportunity for earning income occurs at the same time that school opens. The cost of sending a child to school includes tuition ($10), school uniform and shoes ($25) and classroom supplies ($25, none of which the school provides)—a total of between $50 and $75 or about half the family's income for a month. Deduct what one child could earn harvesting coffee (about $15 a week), and there goes the rest of a month's average income. Just sending one child to school, then, means forfeiting a month's income that frequently does not cover the family's basic necessities to begin with. So the idea of sending all four-to-six children to school is out of the question. In fact, parents of a typical family have absolutely no financial means of sending all their children to school, and at best have to make a tremendous sacrifice to choose even one of their children to attend. These are the factors that keep the poverty-stricken majority of Guatemala's children virtually outside the educational system.

Therefore, helping a child finish the sixth grade means, basically, giving the child and the family the necessary incentive. If the family does not have to pay school costs or worry so much about lost income from the child not working, and if they can remain sufficiently healthy, maybe a child will succeed in school.

To citizens of developed countries like the U. S., this state of affairs might seem overwhelming. How could any child have even the slightest chance of overcoming such great odds? The irony is that at times the only thing a child and family needs is just that—"the slightest chance."

Alma Barrios is a good example. The oldest of three children, Alma lived in San Gaspar with her father Roberto, a construction worker, and her mom, Leonarda. The parents sacrificed greatly to send Alma to elementary school in Antigua. Nevertheless, they prayed that she would continue in junior high school and eventually study for a career. This kind of family support for young women in Guatemala is rare. In Alama's case it was even more unlikely that such dreams would come true since her father suffered from epilepsy that at times made it difficult for him to keep a job. Alma affiliated with Common Hope in the sixth grade, just in time for her to make plans

Alma Barrios, a former sponsored child, was one of the first teachers selected for the Children's Center.

49

for junior high school and, afterwards, to study towards a bilingual secretary career. No doubt she would have succeeded in those plans. However, the course required long hours at a typewriter, and over time the posture irritated a damaged nerve in her neck.

Roberto and Leonarda, undeterred by the setback of their firstborn, helped Alma look for another path. Alma's talents with small children pointed the way. Her parents encouraged her interest in working with preschoolers, but no one knew of any training available for such a career. Roberto set out to investigate. For weeks he searched throughout Antigua and neighboring communities. Finally, he found a little known school nearby that offered training in early childhood education. Common Hope paid half the cost. Leonarda transformed the front room of their house into a convenience store to help meet the additional expenses, and Alma was able to graduate.

The next step for Alma was to find a job, a challenge that fit into larger plans that were already being woven in place. Common Hope's Children's Center would be opening soon. In fact, ten days after her graduation Alma was one of the first to be employed there. Alma said:

> I am a member of the Gethsemene Assembly of God Church. When the church heard about the blessing in my life, they prayed a long time to thank God. We like to sing a lot, so there was lots of singing and clapping, too, since we were so happy with the good news. I love working at the Children's Center. And, of course, I share some of my income with the family. It's my way of saying thanks.

The stories of Alma Barrios and Edi Rodríguez are less about Common Hope than about the initiative and faith of some poor families. Alma and Edi were the kind of children whose latent talents were like jewels lying close to the surface, easily gathered and polished.

But what about children like two-year-old Juan and his three-year-old sister Julia? If their mother, Lupe, had not received timely counseling, she would never have been able to participate in Common Hope's programs. If her children had not received nutritional supplements, they might not have made it to the first grade. And what about Margarita whose teenage son kept stealing from the neighbors? If she had never found an understanding social worker, the whole family might have suffered. (We will take a closer look at Lupe and Margarita in the next two chapters.) These cases were far more characteristic of the families that Common Hope found mired in complex poverty-related problems—chronic illness, no place to study, no electricity, no family support, no solution for learning disabilities or behavioral problems, no transportation, and on and on. Coordinating programs, staff and volunteers to dig through these multi-layered issues was the challenge that demanded a stable environment and space for expanded programs—in short, a Family Development Center.

In spring of 1993 John bought two acres of land from the owner of an old coffee plantation, and then another adjacent acre a few years later. While Kitty managed the day-to-day responsibilities of the Antigua office, John, Kitty and a team of managers organized the construction of the Family Development Center (also referred to as the Antigua site). The primary mission of assisting children's education guided the entire effort. How the construction was designed and completed without losing sight of that goal is a testament to the high level of commitment and vision among the leaders, the staff and volunteers.

It started with volunteers and Guatemalans clearing the underbrush and building a perimeter wall. Armed with suggestions from several volunteer consultants, John developed the site, keeping in mind the future growth needs of the project, the flow of human traffic and an aesthetic mix of simple lines and open green spaces. All buildings would meet California earthquake standards since one of the purposes of the center is to serve as a base for relief operations should catastrophe strike—and it would.

Putting in place a perimeter wall and guardhouse secured the property. Then work began on the first of six major buildings, the vocational school. John started with this building because it was smaller and cost less, and it would serve well as a model to train newly-hired construction workers (the fathers and brothers of affiliated children). In addition, it provided mechanical shops necessary for vehicle and equipment repair.

The second building was the volunteer house that included dormitory space, kitchens and dining facilities. John had planned that, with these two buildings, volunteers and staff could move out of the rented spaces in Antigua, and all the project's needs for housing and programs could finally be located on one site. The order for building the other units simply proceeded south across the three acres, allowing access for delivery of construction materials. (Figure 1: Map, Antigua Site numbers the various structures on the property according to the order in which they were built.)

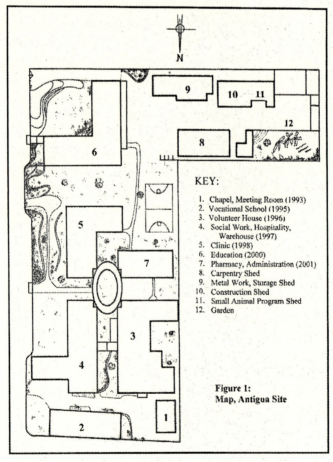

KEY:

1. Chapel, Meeting Room (1993)
2. Vocational School (1995)
3. Volunteer House (1996)
4. Social Work, Hospitality, Warehouse (1997)
5. Clinic (1998)
6. Education (2000)
7. Pharmacy, Administration (2001)
8. Carpentry Shed
9. Metal Work, Storage Shed
10. Construction Shed
11. Small Animal Program Shed
12. Garden

Figure 1:
Map, Antigua Site

Pouring the concrete roof for the vocational building requires a bucket brigade of staff, volunteers, workteam members and family members.

From clearing the property in the summer of 1993 to placing the last blocks in the connecting walkways in the summer of 2001, construction of the Family Development Center took eight years, cost $2.4 million (one fourth the cost of the same construction in the U.S.), put 48,400 square feet under roof and employed at least 75 Guatemalans.

Both the total cost and time involved would have been much higher without the contributions of hundreds of volunteers. To organize the volunteers, Kitty recruited Jewel Anita Hendrix, a former teacher of seven years in Quetzaltenango, to develop a comprehensive program. Jewel Anita provided workteams with orientation to Guatemala culture, discussions with John and other long-term project leaders and a closing session to evaluate and share their learnings.

One of the first workteams included Dorothy Zumwalde from Richmond, Minnesota, in November of 1994. Dorothy, mother of four and grandmother of six, said:

> At my church I attended Dave's presentations about Common Hope and saw the slides of the schools they'd built.
>
> In 1994 my TEC support group sent out a call for carpenters, electricians and whoever else was available to go with us to Guatemala. I gathered funds from Christian Mother's groups, Lions Clubs and others and had an organizational meeting of about 12 people.

Each of us carried on the trip an extra suitcase of supplies from the home office. South of Antigua on the new property, the land had been pretty much cleared, and the walls and first floor of the vocational building had been built. I mixed cement with a hoe and straightened rusty nails for a day or two. Also, I worked in the Antigua office to help with the filing, the laundry and cooking for the workteam. I didn't have a godchild at the time, but while I was there Kitty picked out one for me.

When I returned home I encouraged other groups to go. Many of my friends began to sponsor children. I've been back to Guatemala four times. Hallie, my daughter, served as a long-term volunteer a few years later.

Construction activities were not limited to the project site. No one knew better than Rosa Elena that without protection from damp earth, children would continue to suffer from infections, parasites and respiratory illnesses. Often she "prescribed" floors to prevent these problems. By early 1994 social workers had organized a program that

A North Carolina workteam puts together the first corner of a new family home.

included financial incentive for families to help one another pour concrete floors. The only problem with the floors and the kind of wooden houses built at first was that they were permanent. At times landlords would kick out the families and jack up the rent for new tenants.

Kitty, John, and Adolfo decided to develop a portable, prefabricated house with sheet metal roofing, wood framing and walls of pressed fiber and concrete. Depending on whether the family owned or rented their property, the floor could be poured permanently or laid down in pre-cast squares. In the latter case the entire house and floor could be moved in a day if need be.

By the time the 12' x 16' prototype was built, Kitty, John, Adolfo and the social workers had developed a point system to evaluate the urgency of a family's need for housing. They also drew up a plan that spelled out how the family could pay the cost through sweat equity. The families assisted workteams or staff to construct the houses. This system formed the basis on which a housing committee has continued to build about 50 houses a year. Other projects in nearby towns now use this "culturally appropriate model." (See Figure 2: Family House.)

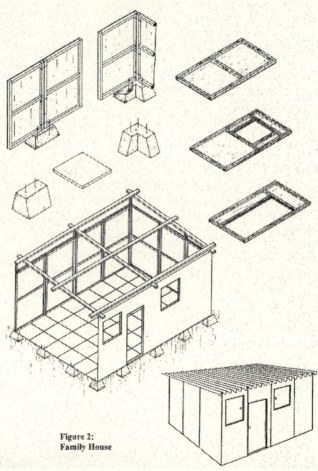

Figure 2:
Family House

These houses not only reduced the incidence of illness, but also encouraged the entire family on a deeper emotional level, especially the children. A construction team on which I participated completed a house in a matter of days for a family with two boys, six and eight

years old. All that remained was to sweep out the sawdust. The boys playfully fought over a broom until we found a second one. Together they swept the floor so clean that the brooms could no longer lift the last particles onto the cardboard they were using as a dustpan. So they crouched on their elbows and knees to pick up the remaining dirt pinch by pinch. Then they ran around inside the

Delfina Choc and her children are proud of their new home, which cost Delfina about 200 hours helping out in Common Hope's clinic. She is now attending junior high school and studies in Common Hope's library several afternoons a week.

house literally bouncing off the walls, something they could never have done previously in their cornstalk shelter. When it came time to bless the house, the two boys wore on their sweaty faces an unforgettable mixture of joy and pride.

Moving into a new house was a thrilling occasion for Guatemalan families. Project workers felt a similar joy when they moved into their new quarters at the Family Development Center in the summer of 1996—a moment arriving none too soon. Staff and volunteers had long outgrown the office on Ninth Street, making it necessary to rent four additional nooks and crannies in Antigua. The occupants had had their fill of muddy boots left in common living areas and little to no privacy. What a relief to be loading some fifty truckloads of desks, computers, boxes and beds and moving into newly constructed facilities.

Complementing these developments in Guatemala was John's re-organization of the home offices in St. Paul. While Dave continued to cultivate the sponsorship program and to make fundraising presentations throughout his seminary years (1992-95), Barb Hansen had been working out of her home office in St. Cloud, MN, and John from a room in St. Paul. Convinced that there had to be something better than this complicated three-way system (all without benefit of e-mail), John called Jay Lyons, a former volunteer and professional in computer science and business administration. He and Joanne Arnold, previously with Habitat for Humanity, developed a new home office that by 1996 had moved into generous warehouse space provided at far below market value by board member Dick Palen.

Having located Common Hope in new space both in St. Paul and Antigua, John arrived at the Family Development Center in late 1995 to receive the baton from Kitty while she became Director of Education. John discovered that his role, clarified a few years back by having taken over as Director from his father, was about to change again. Now he would wear two more hats as Site Director and as Director of Construction. He called 1996 a renaissance year. Indeed, not only was John's role evolving, the whole structure of Common Hope was experiencing a new birth—ample cause for celebrations.

Dave put the responsibility of the sponsorship program in the hands of Jennifer Muyres in the St. Paul office. With his studies behind him, he arrived in Guatemala in February of 1996 to manage the social workers. Eights months later he eloped with nurse Bina Perowitz, a former volunteer and long-time friend. They were married in a Benedictine monastery in Hawaii. They returned to live and work at the project, arriving just in time to attend a 250-person "sit-down dinner" in the project's new dining room. The event celebrated the wedding of long-term volunteers Tom McCullough and Elizabeth Jorda. They were delighted to share the moment with Dave and Bina.

The festive spirit culminated on July 26, 1996, when more than two dozen residents and staff gathered in the narrow parking lot outside the main entrance. After a few words from John and a short prayer by Dave, the assembly opened the entrance door, filed inside and came to a halt in front of the white ribbon stretched across their path. Together Dave and John held a pair of scissors to share in the ribbon cutting. To Ana it seemed as if she were participating in the opening of a giant present on this 26th of July, 1996. It was her birthday.

No one could have been happier than Kitty. Having adopted a child, she and infant Jessie would now have room enough to feel like a family. Kitty was gratified that after her three and a half years as Site Director, the number of children affiliated with the project had more than tripled—from 300 in 1992 to over 900 in 1995. She was glad to be moving into a new position as Director of Education. Now she could focus on the interest closest to her heart—the education of the children. After all, that was, indeed, the heart of the matter.

Dave and John cut the ribbon at the celebration of the beginning of the new Family Development Center.

Heart of the Matter

Having established a sponsorship program, a clinic and a center of operations, John, Dave, Kitty and a core group of managers could now confront more directly the educational needs of the children. The broad range of programs that Common Hope eventually offered to assist children's education did not appear all at once. Rather, the services grew out of what project workers learned as they responded to the children's needs.

To anyone looking at the condition of education in Guatemala the most glaring needs were reflected in poor attendance records and high dropout rates. The failure of 60% of first graders was discouraging, a tremendous waste of resources. Who could understand the matter better than Lorenzo Sipac? As a Guatemalan, he attributed his success in school to the assistance that he had received as a child.

Lorenzo, youngest of six children, had grown up in Patzún, a war-torn Cakchiquel village between Antigua and Lake Atitlán. In the midst of the '76 earthquake his dad rushed back into the rubble of their house to rescue two-and-a-half-year-old Lorenzo. The heroic effort saved the boy, but a falling rafter took his dad's life. When Lorenzo reached school age, his older brother found a childcare agency near Antigua to take care of him. They provided Lorenzo with his room, board and education for years and helped him finish high school. Appreciative of the crucial role that the agency had played in his own education, Lorenzo started looking for work as a teacher and found a position with Common Hope in 1995.

Attendance, Tutoring and Vacation School

Kitty discussed the matter of attendance with Lorenzo, who understood well the problems children were having in school. Many of the difficulties could be traced to the parents' lack of involvement. So Lorenzo immediately initiated a series of home visits to families with children having difficulties at school or at home. He wanted to encourage parents to make sure that their children participated in school and did their homework. It seemed like a lost cause in cases of children who had begun school three months late due to harvesting coffee beans. So in August, using desks in the hallways at the Ninth Street office in Antigua, Lorenzo began helping three students after school with their homework. That number grew to five students in September and ten in October. Sadly, Lorenzo concluded that there would be several of these children who, even with tutoring, would not be able to pass to the next grade. They needed more than tutoring.

Borrowing the primary school in San Pedro, Lorenzo organized the first "vacation school" in November of 1995—four weeks of "basics" for children preceded by a week of teacher training. The local teachers not only enjoyed the extra income that Common Hope paid them for attending the training workshops, but also the imaginative teaching methods taught and modeled by project instructors. They had never been exposed to such creativity in the classroom.

Martha Miza, manager of the primary school program, plays with children during vacation school recess.

Most of all, the kids loved it—the ride in the blue van, Ana's snacks and the creative classroom activities. Volunteer social worker Gerry Carlsen wrote what it was like to go pick up the children in the villages:

> When we arrived, they were jumping up and down and cheering. The mothers standing on the street corners asked if their other children could go, too, because word had gotten around. We originally had 95 kids, and it grew to 120 in three days. After that, we had to say no. Then the mothers came to the office to ask when the next opportunity would be to enroll their children, and we had to say, "Next year." The kids

loved it so much, which is really surprising given that they were the school "failures."

To check up on the effect, if any, that these measures were producing in the students' behaviors, the project's educators and social workers launched a campaign to make sure that every teacher in the public schools attended by children affiliated with the project had an attendance booklet at the start of the school year. Twice a semester project workers returned to collect reports on the students' grades and conduct and then entered the information into the child's records on the computer. They found that the kids' attendance steadily improved and that parents were getting better at encouraging their children. Finally, a trust between Common Hope and the families had developed that would make them partners on behalf of a brighter future for the children.

Gratified by the success of these achievements, Kitty recommended to Lorenzo that he make tutoring a year-round program for first through fourth graders. Beginning in 1996 tutoring moved out of the hallways of project buildings and into village schools. The children, 45 in each school, came for two hours twice a week in the afternoon. Staff and volunteers helped them with their homework and engaged them in conversation about the importance of education, respect for their family and even basic hygiene. By 1998 more than a dozen teachers and volunteers were tutoring four days a week in six schools, reaching more than 400 children. Eventually, the project added tutoring for fifth and sixth graders and held their sessions in the project's new education building. Vacation school, including teacher training, continued to be offered every November. The event expanded to schools in two more villages where 30 or more children always attended.

Special Education

By administering tutoring programs, vacation schools and attendance booklets, the educators themselves learned a great deal in the process. One shocking lesson convinced them that they would have to provide special education to kids like Rosita and Jorge who continued to have problems in school.

Rosita and Jorge were old enough to be fifth graders. However, since they frequently acted out their aggressive impulses, they had never been promoted beyond the second grade. Common Hope transported them to Antigua where the only school available for children with special needs was located. The school had enrolled 40 kids ranging from 6 to 21 years of age. The place was terribly overcrowded, and the children were often left unsupervised during recess—conditions that aggravated Rosita's and Jorge's aggression. Their parents complained to Kitty and Lorenzo who immediately arranged to visit the school. To their horror they found Rosita and Jorge locked in separate closets. They'd been there for hours, a method the school commonly used to punish children who were not behaving well.

Common Hope's education department quickly began organizing its own special education. Even though Common Hope's philosophy is not to duplicate programs that Guatemala already provides, in this case Kitty and the department felt that they had no alternative. However, they did plan to make their "special ed" so successful that the Guatemalan Ministry of Education would integrate it into the public school system.

Kay Lantsberger, an elementary and special education teacher, had heard about Common Hope through a social justice trip to Guatemala with her church. She had planned to take a sabbatical during the very year that Common Hope was looking for help with special education. Kay arrived as a long-term volunteer in July 1997.

Kay went to the public schools and thoroughly researched the children whose problems were affecting their performance. She spent at least one full day testing each child, then selected 40 students who could be best served by the new school. While she trained four teachers and their assistants, temporary classrooms were being constructed on the project grounds. Ready to begin work at the start of the 1998 school year, Kay and her teachers called their program The School of Hope.

Two months into the program eight-year-old Juan Sálazar caught Kay's attention. He had been failing in public school, but Kay thought he was doing just fine in the special program. Kay said:

> I spoke to Juan's social worker about placing him in a private school near where he lived to see if he just needed better attention, not necessarily special education. We found a school for him and spoke to him about how important his education was. Two months later I ran into Juan and his mother. They were reporting his grades to the project and both were beaming. Juan's mother told me that his private school teacher had said that Juan was at the top of his class. And he was smiling ear to ear! I've never forgotten the look on his face. All the hours of work I put in that year were worth it to see those smiles that day.

Children mug for the camera after School of Hope classes are over for the day.

In two years the program became so well known within Guatemala's Ministry of Education, that it won approval as a pilot project to be tested in public schools in San Juan and San Pedro and the following year in Santa Catarina and San Bartólome. Common Hope continued to recruit special education teachers and provide training and salary for two years, before they became government teachers.

When Kay left, Lorenzo became coordinator of the special school. With project funding he enrolled in a five-year course that awards diplomas for Teachers Specialized in Learning Problems. Lorenzo said:

> Like Kay, I am now able to evaluate children to determine if they can benefit from special education. The children's social workers or their public school

teachers refer them to me. I found several children who were failing because of poor hearing, so we employed a speech therapist. I also found 7- to 12-year-olds who had poor physical coordination because they had been severely restricted at home. I am providing them a program to stimulate their motor skills. A seven-year-old came to us barely able to walk but is making rapid progress in our program. Now he runs with the other children and can use a crayon.

Lorenzo Sipac helps children with their school work.

Teacher Training

The quality of Common Hope's teachers as demonstrated in tutoring, vacation school and special education stood out from the Guatemalan norm. Public schools began calling Common Hope for help with teacher training in 1996 when Sandy Everlove arrived with her husband, physician Marcus Remple, and their two children. A high school science teacher from Seattle, Sandy engaged students in science experiments. These activities piqued the interest of project educators who already had been providing training for public school teachers. Since First Aid was one of the subjects in the training curriculum, the educators found a valuable resource in Sandy and Marcus and used their knowledge to explore additional creative methods for teaching science, math and literacy.

Gaining wide respect for their excellence in teacher training, project educators were invited by Guatemala's Council on Reading and Writing to lead workshops at their national and international conferences. By 1999 Common Hope had given workshops on educational methods to over 800 teachers, a figure that doubled in 2000. Guatemala's Ministry of Education recognized Common Hope for providing the kind of changes that improved educational methods and teachers' performance. In 2000 Kitty moved from Director of Education to begin working on developing a national teacher education program. John saw the importance of teacher training stemming from its long-term effect: "When we help a child in education, we help one child. But when we help a teacher improve, we are helping every child who enters that teacher's classroom throughout the teacher's entire career."

Library and Resource Center

Common Hope was committed to improving Guatemala's teachers and schools and not duplicating existing programs by setting up a separate school system. The teacher training provided by Common Hope is a good example of this philosophy in action. In the process it also introduced Guatemalan teachers to instructional resources not found in the Guatemalan schools—overhead projectors, TV/VCRs, computers, games and a variety of printed material. Even a collection of books in public schools was a rare sight. By 1996 the project's few books had grown to several shelves, thanks to an active volunteer book committee at work in the U. S. office. Then with the advent of teacher training, the need for a formal library and educational resource center proved to be an idea whose time had come.

Since a library was a foreign notion to most Guatemalan children, project educators introduced the concept slowly by making "mini-libraries" available during vacation school. The mini-library consisted of a wooden trunk loaded with 50 or more books and carried to the vacation school site. As volunteer "librarian" one year, I spread

Angel Hernández, librarian, gathers children together for a storytelling session.

pieces of carpet on the concrete floor and expected that kids would drop by, choose a book and quietly enjoy it on one of the mats. It rarely happened in that manner. Rather, a pack of children, choosing "reading" over recess, crowded around the trunk as if it were a giant kettle of food. As many hands as possible reached in at once. It dawned on me that most of the children were not looking for any books in particular, but merely wanted to stir them around a bit, literally, to see what they felt like. Checking out a book meant pulling it free from someone else's grip. Once on the mats, the children began loud storytelling from their books, regardless of whether they could read or not. I realized how hungry they were for the stimulation they found in books. The only thing missing was a place to make them available.

Fortunately this need was met by a generous grant from the Perham Rotary Club of Minnesota. Now Common Hope's library and resource center, visited by 50 to 100 kids daily, is the main attraction in the education building. While computers keep track of all books checked out and returned, children use the space for doing homework, enjoying storytellers or communicating with a pen pal through the Internet.

Scholarships and Support Groups

Good news: By the latter half of the 90s Common Hope rejoiced to see an increasing number of its affiliated children graduating from the sixth grade. The assistance being given to kids was working.

More good news: Many of the youth wanted to go on to junior high and even further.

Hard news: Beyond the sixth grade lay a strange new world in schools that were usually farther away from home, more expensive and rife with new adolescent pressures.

Common Hope met these challenges in two ways that worked in tandem—scholarships and support groups (sometimes called youth clubs). Financial aid was available on the condition that the student participate in a support group.

To make sure that scholarship students started out on the right foot, support group leaders brought them together in December, a month before school opened. They wanted students to succeed, so they told them what Guatemalan junior high teachers expected, even how to draw a straight line without smudging the paper. In addition, the leaders taught them how to distinguish between rote learning and a true understanding of their subjects. As a result some students like Eduardo Calderón gained a better understanding of mathematics than the teacher.

Eduardo, the oldest of six children, had helped his dad harvest coffee beans ever since the day he could reach the branches. What

Eduardo liked most was weighing the beans, counting up the money they expected to receive and going to the coffee production center. Eduardo's dad, Pedro, noticed Eduardo's gift with numbers. He and his wife, Gloria, prayed daily that Eduardo might find his way to continue in school. He was their brightest child and was always at the top of his class. Finally, prayer was the only thing left after Pedro broke his leg—the same year that Eduardo graduated from the sixth grade. Instead of going on to junior high, Eduardo had no choice but to take his dad's place in the coffee fields.

Claudia Hernández attended high school on a Common Hope scholarship. At the same time she was responsible for the care of three younger siblings after her mother died. She now holds the trusted position of handling cash for Common Hope in Antigua.

A year later, Gloria was visiting a friend whose family was affiliated with Common Hope. Doing her friend a favor, Gloria answered a knock on the door. A Common Hope social worker asked, "Is there anyone here who could use a scholarship for junior high school?" Gloria, stunned at what seemed like a direct answer to prayer, asked if there might be a scholarship available for Eduardo. Indeed there was, and Gloria and the social worker met later to affiliate Eduardo.

Joining his parents in prayers of thanksgiving, Eduardo went on to finish junior and senior high school, again at the top. Then he found a job managing a plant nursery that required all his mathematical skills and more. Eduardo proved he could count more than coffee beans.

In 1996 when Common Hope first offered scholarships only 15 students participated. Fortunately, these 15, like Eduardo, were so determined to succeed that they made excellent role models for others to follow. The program grew rapidly, so that within five years 600 teenagers were participating. The first ten scholarship students entered college in 2000, and Common Hope continued to pay the cost of their education. Though they were not required to attend support groups or tutoring, some did so on their own. In addition, most of them worked nights, weekends or whenever they could to contribute to their families. Following the example set by the likes of Edi Rodríguez, Alma Barrios and Eduardo Calderón, the youth wanted to pay back their families for having allowed them to go to school for so long.

Adult Education

By the late 90s, educators could look back and see a profound change. Whereas continuing past the sixth grade had been a foreign notion at first, now families expected their children to do this and more. But educators were not the only ones to notice a new day dawning. Parents and other adults saw the positive results of education in their kids' lives and believed that it was never too late to learn.

Common Hope supported the adults' renewed interest in learning to read and write by allowing the time spent in literacy classes to qualify as hours of sweat equity. The number of adults participating in literacy classes varied depending on what was happening in the families' lives. Therefore, social workers played a crucial role in helping adults assess their circumstances to determine whether it would be appropriate for them to enroll.

Adult women and older girls participated more consistently in classes that taught literacy along with sewing skills. Various institutions in Antigua offered sewing classes but required students to have a sixth grade education and sewing machines. Common Hope not only dropped these requirements, but also offered literacy training as part of a three-year course. After a year's progress, students received their own sewing machines that in turn helped them complete their course work. Increasing women's self-esteem and enabling them to be better providers for their families, the classes continue to the present with excellent participation.

Juliana Jiatz, 93, stands in front of the chickens she tends for her extended family.

Adults grew accustomed to Common Hope's method of including classes as part of the program requirements. A series of educational sessions was built into the programs that helped families learn how to raise chickens, grow vegetables and install a more efficient stove. Designed to raise the family income, lower the incidence of eye and respiratory problems and improve the diet, these "family environment" programs contain a four-step process: (1) making an application with the help of their social worker, (2) evaluating their home situation to ascertain the appropriateness of the program, (3) attending a series of classes on the fundamentals of the subject and (4) earning the needed materials through sweat equity. Affiliated families may "buy" any or all of these programs by attending classes or working hours at the project. (One hour of sweat equity was valued at more than the market rate for the same work.)

Several participants, like Virginia González, take advantage of all three programs. The chicken program is the longest running, having been developed by Dave Huebsch in the early years of the project. Virginia and her 15-year-old son, Enrique, learned about water and feed, how to recognize diseases and clean cages. Program leaders helped them construct their own 3' x 6' chicken cage. (See Figure 3: Chicken Cage.) Starting with the 20 chicks provided by the project,

69

Virginia was ready to sell 17 within two months. Three had died. Free-range chickens would have taken six months to grow to this size. She only needed to sell 10 to break even, but she used the profit to invest in another cage and a second batch of 40 chicks. Continuing to re-invest for two years, Virginia eventually tended to more than 300 chickens and built a chicken house on her property.

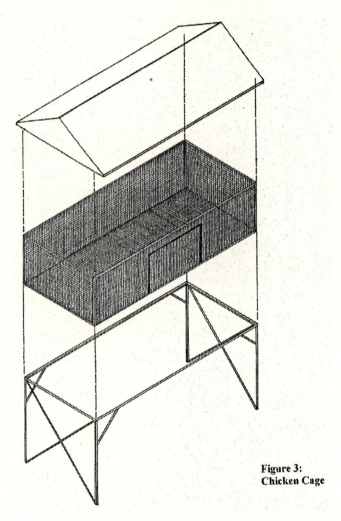

Figure 3:
Chicken Cage

With her extra income, Virginia bought some tools that came in handy for the garden program. As coordinator of the gardening program, I and my assistant, Vilma Luz, taught Virginia and Enrique how to compost, prepare beds for planting according to bio-intensive methods, control pests with organic home remedies and grow herbs useful for a variety of common infirmities.[24] The garden plants that grow the best are the roots (radishes, beets, onions, garlic, carrots), leafy plants (lettuces, chard, celery, cilantro, parsley, spinach) and other vegetables (green beans, chile, cucumber, peppers, zuchini and other squash). Least successful are the tomatoes, potatoes and plants in the cabbage family.

For cultivating medicinal herbs the workshops by Armando Cácerez, Central America's foremost expert in the field, proved essential.[25] His resources helped Vilma and me identify the plants most useful for the common complaints families brought to the clinic—symptoms related to the respiratory system (cough, fever) and the digestive system (stomach pain, diarrhea, parasites). In addition, two herbs that women use to stimulate the flow of breastmilk were frequently cultivated.

Virginia enriched her family's diet with vegetables from her garden and sold the medicinal herbs she raised to the project's pharmacy. Volunteers and women working hours in the gardening program prepared the medicinal herbs into mixtures for teas.

Virginia cooked over an open fire, so she also applied to the stove program. The type of stove she earned and helped build (see Figure 4: Stove) is based on models developed by Larry Winiarski, a mechanical engineer and consultant to many undeveloped countries in wood-burning stoves.[26] In this program each family helps five others in the group construct their stoves. By the end of the process, Virginia and her family had become experts on the use and construction of their stove—a model that burns hotter, uses less wood and vents smoke to the outside. Because it reduces eye problems and respiratory infections it is the most popular item in the sustainable technologies section of the education department.

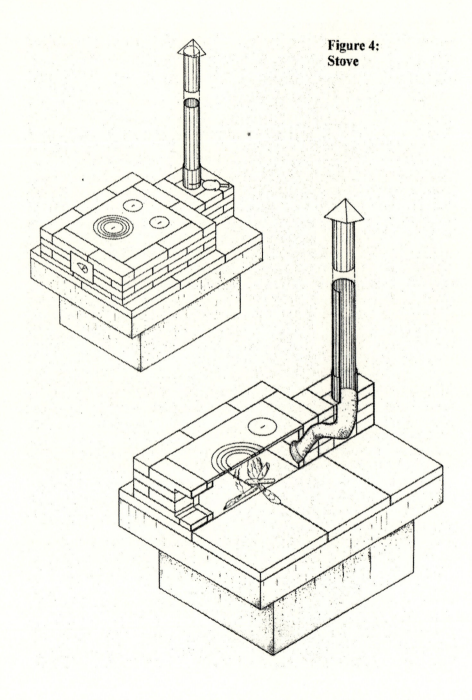

Figure 4:
Stove

Children's Center

On the project grounds the everyday presence of small children created a lively atmosphere. It also increased the risk of accidents when mothers worked their hours of sweat equity while construction was going on. For safety's sake, the project prohibited children from accompanying parents who were working. However, pre-schoolers are very attached to their mothers and vice-versa. The idea of a Children's Center addressed this ongoing tension between safety concerns and local customs. In addition, there was a need to help small children with special problems and a desire to provide daycare for the young babies of staff. Andrea Paret, a former colleague of Kitty's in Habitat for Humanity, said yes to John's and Kitty's invitations to come develop a two-part program providing preschool and daycare options. She arrived from Germany in September, 1998.

Using her experience in nursing, farming and teaching, Andrea thoroughly researched local child care centers and the well-known models from Montessori and Head Start programs. She combined the best of these approaches to design the curriculum for the Children's Center. The program consisted of a preschool for 3- to 5-year-olds (20 kids) and a day care for infants to 6-year-olds (25 kids). Preschool children were chosen because of special needs. They committed for a year or until the child "graduated" into a kindergarten in one of the villages. Daycare provided help for parents who were working hours, attending classes or coping with emergency situations.

Preschool children enjoy playing with a pint-sized replica of the safe and healthy stove their parents can receive.

After training the staff Andrea opened the doors in November 1999, but she found that mothers were

73

reluctant to leave their children at the center. In fact, some relatives would not allow the mothers to use the services or would scold them if they did so. It became apparent that a good but unfamiliar program was coming into conflict with the local custom of women being expected to care for their own children at all times. Common Hope wanted to develop a relationship of deeper trust with the families.

These issues emerged dramatically in relation to the Margón family. They had begun affiliating their children in 1995. However, over the years the family seemed to experience more defeats than victories. The father's alcoholism effectively insulated him against any rehabilitative services that the social workers offered. The mother, Lupe, was a variant of the classic woman who lived in a shoe. She had so many children (fourteen) that in order to cope she did what she felt she had to do. The clinic would give her powdered milk for her children, but she'd sell it and come back for more. The children were seldom in school and always needed medicine, another item not reaching its intended goal.

Finally, in consultation with staff colleagues and Lupe's social worker, Andrea decided that the center could not in good faith continue giving out food, medicine and services that were not helping the family. So she told Lupe that to keep her family's affiliation, it would be mandatory for her to bring her two- and three-year-old children (Juan and Julia) to the pre-school every day without fail. The kids were in dire need of nutritional supplements, regular check-ups and supervision. Andrea tells what happened:

> It was an ultimatum that we put to Lupe Margón. Fortunately, this time she met the challenge. At first, Juan and Julia cried the whole time. Then they found toys, playmates and activities that interested them. When Lupe couldn't bring them, she'd find a neighbor to help. Lupe began attending parents' meetings, and she quit looking down at her feet all the time. Her smiling countenance is now a welcomed presence in the project, especially among those who have known her for a long time.

I took photos of Juan and Julia, when they first came and again two months later, and the difference is like night and day. The paths these two children are taking, and will take in the future, may have been impossible without our rather tough intervention at this early age. Already Lupe's older children have been inspired to improve their school attendance. Who knows, maybe these are the kinds of repercussions that will even reach the father.

Slowly, trust between families and the staff grew, and the Children's Center became a popular place for children to prepare for the first grade and spend creative moments away from their mothers.

Before Andrea left she chose one of the Guatemalan workers to take the position as director of the center. The long-range plan was not to expand child care services at the project, but to train parents to provide child care in local communities. Then the job for the center's staff would be to supervise community-based centers.

A summary of the education department's mission was well stated by César Moreno, the Guatemalan Director who followed Kitty in that position. He said, "If a family comes to us requesting that we install a sewer line for them, we've failed that family. However, if they come asking us to help them find the resources to put in their own sewer line, we've succeeded. The ultimate goal of education is to empower the whole family."

The education department, beginning with the sponsored child, always keeps in sight the siblings, the parents and teachers. However, individual family members are also part of community networks and environmental systems. Taking into account these larger contextual factors, educators join hands with health and social workers every step of the way. Let's now take a look at this bigger picture through the eyes of the clinic and social work department.

Curing and Caring

Let's face it. Living in Guatemala can be dangerous to life and health. Besides the unpredictable (erratic driving, earthquakes and hurricanes), very predictable factors also create hazardous conditions. A 36-year civil war not only taught an entire generation violent methods of "resolving" conflict, but also gave them tons of firearms. As a result, the leading cause of death among both adolescents and adults in Guatemala is firearms and other externally inflicted injuries.[27]   However, pneumonia, intestinal infections and malnutrition are just as dangerous and cause the most deaths among preschool children.[28] These medical factors would not be so lethal if poverty were not so widespread[29] and if the people could get to a clinic or hospital. But Guatemala has the unhappy distinction of being the Central American country with the least available health care: "40% of the population does not have access to health services."[30] The percentage covered by vaccination against common diseases is the lowest in Central America and the Caribbean and even lower than the average among all developing nations.[31]   In Central America Guatemala ranks low in the number of doctors available and comes in last place for the number of hospital beds per 1,000 population. Of its 43 national hospitals, Guatemala's Ministry of Health admits that 65 to 80 per cent are old and on the verge of collapse.[32]

Volunteer social worker Gerry Carlsen described what it was like in a Guatemala City hospital when she accompanied parents to pick up their child, Byron. He had spent the night there to receive treatment for snakebite.

> I left the parents outside and asked if I could see Byron. I followed a staff person who first looked in the emergency room and couldn't find him. We went from ward to ward, but the nurses had no Byron. The smell of urine was so strong I could barely stand it. In the hallways people lay on metal gurneys with no pads or

sheets and called for attention. It looked like there had been a war. A nurse wove in and out between the gurneys carrying a bedpan filled to the brim with blood. There was blood spattered on the walls and floor, and everything was dirty. Byron was not in any of the departments, and I was freaking out. Finally, when we returned to emergency, we found him there. I am now certain I have seen hell.

The poor cannot receive health care if they can't get to it. That is their main obstacle, no access. What happens to families living in the gullies in cases of serious illness? How do they find the help they need?

Curing: Accessible Health Care

From the beginning Common Hope's leaders concerned themselves with the health of the children and their families. Dave and Betty in Atitlán not only built schools but also supported nutrition centers. Their schools provided hot meals for children who came on empty stomachs. In Antigua the combination of Dave's teaching background and John's growing interest in health care further insured that educational goals would always be pursued in the context of the overall health of the child and family.

Little Shirley plays outside the clinic after receiving treatment for a burn.

The Huebsches' first contact in Antigua was Doctor Rosa Elena Solís. She provided medical care for the children referred to her at the Belén project, assembled a small staff at the Ninth Street office and finally helped organize the first clinic and pharmacy at the Family Development Center. One of her earliest accomplishments was to identify leaders in the villages who agreed to attend weekly two-hour classes on preventive health care. By year's end, they had graduated as "health promoters." Presently 14 health promoters serve in the four villages where they live. They keep an eye out for health risk factors such as unsafe sewage runoff. In cases of snakebite and other such emergencies they can give first aid. They disseminate information on hygiene, nutrition and the use of herbal medicines prepared by the project. Their training and presence in the communities make valuable health resources available to the people.

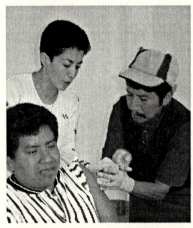

Dr. Rosa Elena instructs village health promoters in how to give shots.

From the original base of operations in Antigua, Dave, John and Kitty put in place an on-call system by which staff and long-term volunteers respond to emergencies at any hour, day or night. Kitty organized the first educators and social workers to make presentations in the villages on health themes. They also held an annual Family Day to give skits on nutrition and hygiene and to distribute anti-parasite medicines. Now leaders in the new clinic provide preventive medicine courses to teachers and social workers and integrate various health themes into existing courses offered by the project's departments.

In these ways Common Hope makes primary care available to thousands in remote villages who previously had no access to these health services. Today the majority of family members who pass through the project's doors are seeking medical attention.

The Clinic

The clinic is equipped with an emergency room for minor procedures, several examining rooms, a pharmacy, dental offices, a nutrition program, eye examination area and a general reception lobby. With the project's transportation system, the doctors may refer patients to hospital emergency rooms in Antigua or Guatemala City or to specialty clinics when necessary.

The clinic has grown from Rosa Elena and her nurse assistant to four doctors (one of whom is the health program director), two nurses, one pharmacy technician, a dentist, a nurse/laboratory technician, a nutritionist and two secretaries, all of whom are Guatemalan. Several volunteers (nurses, physician's assistant, eyeglass technician, etc.) fill out a staff of approximately 15 persons within the clinic.

Patients seen in the clinic suffer generally from infectious diseases—respiratory infections, diarrhea, pneumonia, throat infections, fevers, intestinal parasites and infections of the ears, eyes and skin. Over the decade of the 90s the incidence of these did not change significantly. In recent years, however, the clinic has treated more patients with problems associated with hypertension, musculo-skeletal dysfunction, diabetes and gynecological disorders. To some extent these additional categories reflect the fact that, with more doctors on staff, the clinic has a greater range of diagnostic and treatment capacity.

Consistently the clinic has organized its services in a twofold manner: to provide direct and immediate patient care and to teach families what they can do to prevent illness and enjoy better health. As a result the families take a Band Aid when they need one, but they also learn behavior that in the long run improves their health and reduces the number of their visits to the clinic.

The Clinic Director, Doctor Gustavo Estrada, found through his studies that, generally speaking, the root causes of the problems presented by patients are the social and economic conditions in which they live. For this reason he expects that the clinic will continue to develop programs in preventive medicine and public health in order to promote a healthier living situation. Rosa Elena totally agrees. "These educational programs work," she said. "In the early 1990s we had some children who died of malnutrition. Not any more." The nutrition program is one major reason why this is so.

In Latin America 13 children die each hour of malnutrition, the principle cause of death of children under five.[33] To address this glaring symptom of poverty, nutritional supplements were invented in the 1950s by a Guatemalan biochemist who helped organize a five-

79

year master's program in nutrition. Mayarí Dengo graduated from this program and served as the first licensed nutritionist at Common Hope. She and volunteers working in the nutrition program usually receive from the doctors about seven patients a day who suffer from malnutrition or need special dietary consultation. Nutritionists keep records of height, weight and the type of supplement the family receives. In addition, they prepare lessons on proper nutrition for pregnant mothers and diabetics, who attend a series of five monthly

Women learn about nutrition through a bingo game led by long-term volunteer nutritionists Cris Alonso and Angie Palmer.

sessions. Doctors also refer mothers to these groups if their newborn babies are not gaining weight on schedule. If low weight gain is caused by breastfeeding problems, methods including herbal teas are used to help stimulate the flow of breast milk. Formulas can then be used as a supplement to breast milk and not as a substitute.

The nutrition program is symbolic of the direction the clinic as a whole will take in the future—namely, to bring the message and methods of preventive health care to the people. The clinic continues to seek a variety of ways to increase awareness of prevention by making regular presentations to community groups, school health programs, family counseling agencies and training programs for paramedics. Such a

Elaine Happ, a short-term volunteer optometrist, tests a child's vision.

multidisciplinary approach, according to Dr. Gustavo, is how they reached a little girl like Ingrid García.

Ingrid, 11 years old, had trouble focusing her eyes on her homework. Her social worker assisted the family to wire the house for better lighting and to vent smoke to the outside. These measures helped some, but the problem persisted. A health promoter told Ingrid that she ought to have her eyes examined at Common Hope, but Ingrid was too busy preparing for the arrival of her sponsor, Elaine Happ from Monticello, MN. When Elaine visited their home, she heard about the difficulty Ingrid was having in reading. She, too, asked Ingrid to come to Common Hope for an eye exam. Elaine, an optometrist, was waiting for Ingrid with examining equipment and two large trunks of spectacles donated by the Monticello Lion's Club. Ingrid learned that her problem was mainly nearsightedness and was overjoyed to hear that with glasses she would be able to do her homework properly. She was moved to tears to receive her eyeglasses and the gift of better sight from Elaine, her very own godmother. Who knows what kind of potential health and behavioral problems a caring godparent prevented with a simple pair of eyeglasses?

Surgical Teams

Not all health problems are as easy to solve as Ingrid's. Cleft lips and palates, hernias, constricting scars, infected tonsils and adenoids, cysts and tumors are part of a long list of conditions that require surgery. Fortunately, among Common Hope's first board members were several medical professionals—Mike Menzel (anesthesiologist), Warren Schubert (plastic surgeon) and Naomi Quillopa (registered nurse). These three formed a leadership core for the medical teams. They found that it was quite easy to recruit other health care professionals and support staff who were willing to travel to Guatemala at their own expense.

Since 1992 they have come every year to Guatemala to perform a variety of surgeries. The first visit took place in Antigua at a local private hospital. In the mid-90s the group set up surgical units in a rural village and later at a nearby town. In 1998 the team began making two trips—a January event in Antigua and another in February at the Behrhorst facility in nearby Chimaltenango.

In preparation for the arrival of medical teams, announcements are made on the radio and through networks available to the host hospital and local doctors. Screening and follow-up of patients are also done through local offices. On several trips it was necessary to convert empty rooms to a functioning surgical center complete with anesthesia, sterilization and recovery room. It was common for the teams to bring their own water and generators for back-up electricity. All of the equipment they needed to set up a complete surgical unit was inventoried and stored in Common Hope's warehouse after each trip.

Surgical teams have always worked together with local Guatemalan doctors. In this way everyone benefits from the exchange of medical information and skills. Common Hope's clinic staff not only refers patients to its own surgical teams, but also coordinates surgeries with other teams such as those of Faith in Practice from Houston, Texas. Common Hope has supported Faith in Practice's plans to provide a shelter (House of Faith) that will house out-of-town surgical patients and their families.

Time constraints and other limitations require the medical teams to schedule surgeries that do not involve extensive outlays of hospital services. While most cases require one- or two-day hospital stays, twenty percent of the patients are "same-day surgeries" who recuperate just fine at home under the care of their own families and physicians.

Mike Menzel said that one reason he volunteers is to bring medical care where it is least expected and most needed. "I was amazed at the number of burns that people walk around with simply from having to live so close to open

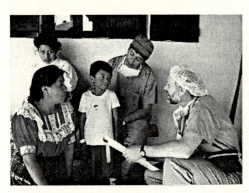

Dr. Mike Menzel, anesthesiologist, consults with a patient prior to surgery.

fires all the time," he said. Mike remembers fondly the patient who brought a bit of humor to the scene:

> We fixed a hernia for Francisco, a twenty-year-old boy who said he was a rock star. Before the operation Francisco entertained us with his electric guitar in the shape of a leaping deer. Afterwards, he continued to perform even from his bed. He told us, "I want you to operate on me again. I've got another hernia." We thought he was just enjoying his medication too much. But sure enough, he did have a hernia on the other side. We operated again, and Francisco stayed another week playing his deer-shaped guitar.

The medical teams' reward is always the patients' heartfelt appreciation. Malnourished three-year-old Estuardo struggled through his cleft lip operation. But every year since his surgery he and his dad have traveled five hours on a bus to come back and thank the medical teams.

Caring: Compassionate Social Work

In the ravines behind the village of Hermano Pedro where Dr. Rosa Elena had first introduced Dave and John to the local people, the retaining walls of mattress springs and chicken wire were no match for the tons of water dumped by Hurricane Mitch that first weekend of November 1998. The father of one of Common Hope's affiliated families, who was also the community's mayor, drowned trying to help others cross the torrents of gushing muddy water and debris.

First to respond to families and communities in crisis were the Common Hope social workers. Pat Campbell, Director of the Social Work Department, wrote to former volunteer Gerry Carlsen a few days after the hurricane:

> Gerry, the water is starting to seep back into people's homes. The social workers worked like

animals yesterday. I don't think I have ever seen dirtier people in real life! The pump blew up on them a couple of times. Two of them looked like they had been standing next to an oil gusher, like in the movie *Giant*!

Today I sent the social workers to fan out to as many families as possible to spread the word about cholera risk and to hand out little bags of clorox. They are identifying immediate needs like mattresses as well as longer-term needs like new beds when they can get back in their homes. We delivered lunch to two shelters yesterday and one today. I had to buy a casket for a month-old baby that died this morning.

I'd better run. It's time for our daily meeting to get the troops organized and sent out.

By the time of Hurricane Mitch, Pat had spent almost two years developing the social work department. The hurricane brought out the very best in them. In this correspondence to Gerry, she called the social workers "troops," an apt characterization of those who fan out, identify needs and take action. But who were they? They had in fact appeared in every phase of Common Hope's history. In the early years they were the ones who had said proudly, "We do everything— build houses, help with funerals, respond to emergencies. You name it." Adolfo had been in charge of them for a while in Antigua, then Dave at the new project site after he had finished seminary, and then Pat.

Empowering Communities and Families

The abiding mission of social work is to make sure that the families receiving services become more self-sufficient—a fundamental part of Common Hope's philosophy from the beginning. Social workers had begun accumulating experience in empowering families' self-sufficiency by organizing women's support groups. They helped women in poor communities identify their own needs as well as the steps they might take to meet those needs.[34] Teaching families the necessary skills to reach their goals involved inventive training sessions such as skits that posed a hypothetical problem for the participants to solve on their own.

By early 1994 a sufficient number of women in San Gaspar were eager to start a women's group. By 1997 additional women's support groups had begun in other villages and a men's group in San Miguel. Two or three leaders in every group came together to discuss leadership skills. One thing they quickly learned was to avoid focusing on money-raising goals at first, even though money was usually uppermost in the minds of the participants. Issues around money within a poor community proved too hot to handle and tended to close a group down. The more successful groups found needs that brought them together in a unified effort. In September of 1994, Gerry Carlsen wrote about one such event:

> My women's group successfully pulled off a wonderful clean-up campaign in their village. They visited every house with the mayor and a representative from the health department to ask people not to throw garbage in the streets and to help pay for a garbage truck to collect weekly. (They never had this service before.) Then the mayor called a "faena," an event in which he "drafts" the responsible male of each household to labor for the good of the village for a day. We had the public clean-up day last Sunday. It's been exciting to see the women grow into being able to carry this off.

The community support groups eventually were organized under the care of the social work department. They continue to serve as models that demonstrate what it means to become more self-reliant.

Healthy communities, in turn, are built on strong, independent families. Parents learn as soon as possible from a Common Hope social worker that their ultimate goal is to "graduate" from the project and not remain dependent on its services. This message is communicated through a teaching game that social workers use with the families. The game, called Step by Step, helps the families set their goals and identify the resources necessary to find solutions.

Social worker Gerry Carlsen makes a call on Marta Julia and her children.

Social worker Sharon Dohse helped Margarita find resources for her family by playing Step by Step. Having already developed a trusting relationship with Margarita, Sharon opened the game board that had over 40 pictures located around the border: eyeglasses, light bulbs, chickens, tools, children studying, etc. Margarita was just beginning to learn to read, but she easily understood the meaning of the pictures. Each represented a goal available to Margarita either through the project's programs or Margarita's resources within herself, her family or community. Margarita's task was to choose the picture cards that she felt best expressed her family's needs. Then she placed those cards on the "family path" in the center of the board. The winding path is a series of connected boxes leading to the symbol of a graduation cap and a handshake. After Margarita had placed the cards on the path, she could see at a glance the steps that she and her family needed to take to reach the goal of increased self-sufficiency.

An interesting thing happened during the game. Margarita was learning that she could find order in the midst of poverty's chaos. The realization came as such a relief to Margarita that she cried and began telling Sharon for the first time about the abuse in her family.

Sharon could see that there were additional factors in Margarita's life that needed attention, factors not represented by pictures on the game board. So she didn't finish the game with Margarita in that session. Rather, she referred her to a psychologist on staff, an important part of the overall plan for Margarita. The game had served a deeper purpose by encouraging openness between a family member and a social worker. From the fertile ground of trust all other services would grow.

As Sharon requested, Margarita brought her husband, Carlos, and three of their children to the next appointment. Sharon's objective was to involve the entire family in reaching its goals, and the game proved to be an excellent strategy to this end. It was especially important for the children to place their "school" and "study" cards on the game

Newly affiliated parents learn how to use the "Step by Step" game to set family goals.

board—goals shared by family and project alike. In addition, Margarita wanted a family more united by bonds of affection. She handed the "united family" card to Carlos for him to place on the game board. Before the session ended, Sharon discussed the symbols at the end of the family's path. The graduation cap meant that the family's relationship with the project would culminate one day, not in a literal graduation ceremony, but in a moment in which the family would become independent of the project. The handshake beneath the cap promised the project's support and celebration of the goals the family reached.

Leonel and Delfina García were able to graduate from Common Hope after they opened a successful village store.

In time, the sessions with families using Step by Step became a standard tool of the social work department after trust was well developed between the family and the social worker. It helps families make plans for the year ahead instead of always being mired in the everyday drudgery of poverty. These sessions with their social workers empower families by increasing their self-confidence, identifying basic resources and mobilizing the entire family toward achievable goals.

Professional Development

Pat worked years to develop "empowering skills" in the social workers. She drew on long experience with the principles of management consulting. [35] Starting out, Pat realized that her "troops" were following the Guatemalan custom of waiting to be told what to do. So her first step in developing the department was to help them get used to taking initiative. She encouraged them to propose ideas in order to set up departmental standards and keep proper records in the distribution of shoes, school supplies and nutritional supplements. It took a year and a half to put departmental procedures in place and develop a good "documentation mentality."

After the hurricane Pat began focusing on broader issues of professional development. She asked a colleague to find ways for social workers to think together about their professional self-esteem. This resulted in the formation of an advisory group to identify basic tasks that all social workers needed to be able to do—how to deal with alcoholism, how to write up and present a case study or how to make an action plan with the family.

The social worker's efforts to help a family develop a plan for itself had sparked the idea of the Step by Step game. In an advanced version of the game families figured out how to resolve issues in fictitious family scenarios, similar to the first women's support groups. As a result, families learned to take the initiative to make their own plans in response to their needs rather than waiting until things got so bad that they would have to call the project for help with an emergency. The fact is that in the present day the project receives far fewer emergency calls than it did earlier in its history when there were fewer families—an achievement that obviously benefits the entire project.

By 2001 the social work department had developed its own identity and respected role in the project's mission, creating an opportune moment to take advantage of further professional development offered by staff psychologists. They led the department employees in discussions on empathy, confidentiality, ethics, sexuality and boundaries. They also taught them the difference between psychological disorders and "a case of the nerves" (a catchall category used in Guatemala to refer to any behavior that seems emotionally strange).

Employment Assistance

In helping families find the resources they need, a social worker invariably discovers that one of the main goals that a family wants to work on is finding a better job. The issue becomes more complicated because the local agriculture-based economy is changing to one of tourism and small industry. As a result many families who had been farming for generations find themselves in a strange new world. Not only do adults have few skills for the emerging economy, they also have little know-how when it comes to finding jobs. For this reason, Common Hope challenged the social workers to create an employment training and referral program (PODER).

An independent management consultant serving as a long-term volunteer was paired with Common Hope's Guatemalan human resources manager. Together they set out in the spring of 2001 to create a job employment agency that within two years would become the agency of choice among many local businesses. They did not want to compete with the government's Ministry of Work, but to create a resource available specifically for the project's affiliated families.

Their first task was to visit local business people to see what kind of employees they wanted and to encourage them to call PODER when they needed to fill a job opening. Job descriptions from local businesses usually specified that the applicant be male, between 25 and 40 years old, with a family, without alcohol problems and preferably with a diploma from the ninth grade. These were tough standards, but within six months the PODER staff had convinced 23 business owners to use the program when searching for applicants.

In the meantime, assembling a corps of job seekers from among affiliated families became the primary focus. The challenge would be more than simply matching people's skills with the right job. Rather, people needed training to develop enough self-confidence to follow through with the job application process. Therefore, a series of Saturday classes was created to enable everyone who entered the program to prepare for the job search and the work environment.

Fernando Méndez entered the program, but not without some skepticism. Just 20 years old, he had learned the hard way how to make it on his own. He did not know his family and often slept in doorways along the street when he had to. When he entered the PODER program he needed only three more semesters to graduate from high school and was determined to do so. Incredibly, he had put himself through school a little at a time by doing odd jobs. He probably never would have come to PODER had he not been attacked and robbed of his only possession—his bicycle. Common Hope stretched its rules a bit to admit Fernando to the program.

The first of five classes in the PODER employment training course dealt with "self-knowledge." Fernando's list of his positive attributes was longer than any of the other participants. His expectations were specific—get a job, graduate from high school, get a better job, raise a family.

In the "search" phase, PODER trainers shared with him a list of job announcements but emphasized the value of using his own network of personal contacts through family and friends. Unfortunately, Fernando had no family, and his many acquaintances knew him as someone who lived in the streets—not the greatest reputation to have when looking for a job. Fernando needed something more than his familiar face and easy chatter. He needed a résumé that would back him up as he put his best foot forward.

The "preparation" class helped him do just that, and his résumé was quite impressive. It included the schools he had attended, his work history (welder, bicycle repairman, gardener, parking attendant, etc.) and his goals.

Fernando needed hardly any instruction on the "interview" session since his personality was always confident, warm and full of good humor. However, following up an interview with a thank you note and telephone call was a novel idea. When Fernando did this, he really impressed his future employer.

During the final "job" phase, PODER directors called the employer to make sure that each new worker was receiving proper orientation on the job and that the employer was satisfied with the performance of the new PODER employee. In Fernando's case his résumé fit exactly the position posted from a local hotel—someone to be a handyman and attend to a range of details from gardening to handling the guests' luggage. Fernando's friendly face at the hotel entrance created a hospitable atmosphere that greatly pleased the hotel manager. With an empty room in the hotel to call his own, Fernando was again on his path to reach his goals.

In addition to Fernando, a total of 35 members of affiliated families were enrolled in the initial PODER classes. Two-thirds of them finished the course, and almost two-thirds of these "graduates" found jobs. Several business people in Antigua now speak from experience when they say that PODER at Common Hope is the first place they call in their search for job applicants. In less than a year the program managers had reached a goal that they thought would take them two years.

Integration of People and Services

On a daily basis Common Hope's staff and volunteers are constantly challenged to keep in mind not only the needs of their families and communities but also their own limits as educators, healers or guides. The process of understanding oneself as a change agent within a society that itself is in dire need of change is called "integration."[36] The term is an apt description not only for the personal awareness of professional helpers but also for the way families and communities think about themselves. Common Hope seeks to build integrated individuals, families and communities—a goal that, in turn, requires the integration of a variety of services. The concept of integration is best understood as it is seen in action. Let's look at what finally happened to Margarita and her family.

I met Margarita when she participated in the gardening program. On our visits to help Margarita dig beds for her garden, Vilma, my assistant, noticed that Margarita's husband was never at home. She said it was a good sign that he had probably quit drinking and gone to work. The bad news was that Margarita was rarely at home either. Her neighbors said Margarita had taken up the drinking habit, leaving the children to fend for themselves. Vilma and I sought the counsel of Sharon Dohse, the family's social worker, who helped us understand Margarita's situation.

Life for Margarita plodded on as one sad drama after another. She'd given birth to sixteen children, nine of them living. Some of them had begun to act out—faking illnesses, getting arrested and such. Eventually, the family had to move when one of the sons was caught stealing from a neighbor. This was particularly distressing to us since it meant that the garden we had dug had been abandoned.

Vilma and I never suspected such a dreary background since Margarita's demeanor was always so friendly. She actively participated in many programs at the project.

But Sharon saw beneath the surface appearances. She read Margarita's constant talk about herself and her busyness at the project as addictive behavior. Perhaps Margarita was using the project's programs mainly to distract herself from her miseries.

Sharon also saw that Margarita was an incredibly strong person in many ways. If only Margarita believed in her own strength. So Sharon decided to help Margarita focus on that strength. She referred Margarita to a Common Hope psychologist and to a support group. At the same time she limited Margarita's presence at the project to the literacy program and helped her control her idle chatter that only served to reinforce a negative self-image. Basically, Sharon was teaching Margarita how to set boundaries and to rely on her strength instead of escapist habits.

Then Sharon got to work on Margarita's most urgent problems with her children. She sent the hearing-impaired child to Common Hope's speech pathology program. With a hearing aid, he totally changed his behavior in school. Turning to the middle boy when he was released from prison, she helped him enroll in a carpentry school program.

"Guess what?" Sharon asked me one day. "Margarita finally graduated from the sixth grade."

This great news from the literacy program reminded me that I had not seen Margarita in a long time. Sharon explained that Margarita was spending more time at home with her children.

Sharon's work often left her emotionally exhausted. In Margarita's case she had integrated a variety of resources from the project's clinic, social work and education departments and from the community. She had taught Margarita how to use a crisis as an opportunity. Most of all she had given Margarita valuable lessons in boundaries and self-reliance. Sharon had woven a variety of resources in and out of the lives of Margarita and her family. As a result the family had become more closely knit to one another and better integrated in their community.

Little Dulce María told her social worker that she was practicing to be a university student.

Common Hope's social workers, like Sharon, dedicate themselves to empowering families. Such families enjoy a greater sense of self-reliance and are far more likely to support their children in school. But even this goal has its limits—especially when disaster strikes.

Zach Thomas

Part Three: Future Designs

Zach Thomas

Hope from a Hurricane

Renato Westby, born in 1973 in Guatemala City, never knew his dad. He lived with his mom until he was five and found her in the middle of the night, dead from pneumonia. A great aunt took him and his older brother, Mario, to an orphanage. Eight months later a Minnesota couple adopted the two boys and raised them in Minneapolis. By 1995 Renato was a university graduate with a major in government and a minor in Spanish.

Since Renato wanted to travel to Central America after his graduation, his mom suggested that he talk with John Huebsch, Executive Director of Common Hope. She knew about the project through her friend, Barb Hansen, who had managed the U. S. office in the early years. Reflecting on his meeting with John at a restaurant next to Common Hope's offices in St. Paul, Renato later said, "Having supper with John was the best decision I ever made. A few months later in March of 1996 I was building houses for the poor in Guatemala."

Eric Carpenter grew up in Fergus Falls, MN, and entered the same university as Renato. He wanted to become a corporate lawyer, but changed his mind after working with the homeless in Mexico during a January term his freshman year.

A year behind Renato, Eric finished college and decided to teach math and algebra to displaced students along the border of Belize and Guatemala. In Belize a friend suggested that he look up Renato at Common Hope during his Christmas vacation in Antigua. Eric ended up staying longer in Antigua to work at Common Hope. He made such an impression that John invited Eric to come back after his stint in Belize. Eric returned in August of 1997, and by October Renato had trained him as a manager of Common Hope's housing construction.

Working in a variety of roles taught both of the recent graduates a broad range of new skills. Renato learned how to build efficient stoves, repair computers and examine eyes to fit people for proper glasses. Eric jumped into car mechanics, phone installation and electrical systems. They laughed upon discovering that back in college they'd missed meeting each other because they had skipped the same Spanish class. Soon, however, they would sit together in a course taught by the sternest teacher they'd ever had—Hurricane Mitch.

The first weekend in November, 1998, Mitch came through Central America, the deadliest hurricane in more than 200 years and tying for fourth among the strongest ever recorded in the Atlantic basin. While Guatemala suffered fewer people killed and wounded than the neighboring countries, thousands of its people were left homeless and economically devastated. Those living on steep hillsides not only lost their homes but also their hope of ever rebuilding. The land on which they had once lived either no longer existed or had been forever reconfigured into impossible cliffs by five days of nonstop rain.

At Common Hope, Eric and Renato organized teams of eight people. Within a couple of months they'd finished building or repairing at least a house a day in the villages served by Common Hope. The lesson Mitch was teaching them was not housing construction. They'd already passed that course. Mitch was teaching them about land—assessing it, grading it, retaining it and draining it.

The final exam came when a representative from a Catholic charities group, Caritas, called John. The official had seen the houses that Common Hope was building. He told John about a parish in Guatemala City whose members' houses had been washed off the side of a steep hill. He wanted Common Hope to help them re-build. Knowing he still had money donated for disaster relief, John agreed to see what could be done.

Soon John and Eric found themselves standing on the edge of a precipice with the parish priest, looking at an area that once had been a neighborhood of his parishioners. Now it resembled a garbage dump at the bottom of a deep ravine. Both John and Eric knew instantly that the steep, sandy hillside should never be covered with houses again. Eric lifted his eyes to the plateaus beyond and in passing said, "We *could* build on something like that."

John was so moved by the desperate conditions of the people that he began to keep his eyes open for land. Within weeks the priest called to say that one of his parishioners was willing to sell some land. In early 1999 John, Eric and Renato traveled northeast of Guatemala City to visit a rural site owned by various members of a Guatemalan family. By the spring of 1999 Common Hope had begun purchasing parcels that within a year would total 34 acres. The additional good news was that there would be room for displaced families from several ravine communities around Guatemala City. What an opportunity made possible by donations for victims of Hurricane Mitch!

Beautifully hidden in pastoral countryside, the property resembles a thumb and forefinger pointing northeast and outlined by steep gullies. Rising from a neighboring stream bed to the east is a third peninsula on top of which the Sisters of the Eucharist had built a

The first homes built in New Hope village await the improve-ments that residents and Heart of Hope will provide.

home for abandoned women. One passes by their facility to enter Common Hope's newest project site.

In brainstorming ideas for how to develop the property, John, Eric and Renato looked for existing models and never found a match. Creating an intentional village of families, most of whom did not know one another, seemed to be a new concept.

How would the families be chosen to live there? Where would the children go to school? What kind of transportation, medical and social services were available? Fortunately, Common Hope could draw from years of tending to family and community development to address these questions. To get started on a new model of housing construction, John contacted Kip Scheidler, Habitat for Humanity's director of special programs in Latin America. He agreed that Habitat and Common Hope could create a joint venture, first of a kind for Common Hope. Habitat would fund the housing while Common Hope would develop the land and oversee the project. Families would become homeowners by building each other's houses and paying off small mortgages to Habitat. They would earn the title to their land from Common Hope in exchange for hours of community work over a five-year period. Thus, for their sweat equity families would receive not just a house and land but a whole village—New Hope Village, the name Renato suggested.

Such plans called for decisions that would have both immediate and long-term effects. Renato was already making commitments for his own future. He married Guatemalan Lourdes López, and the couple eventually settled onto the new property as their first home.

Eric, on the other hand, knew that he would be returning to the U.S. soon. In the year before his departure, he directed housing construction at both Antigua and New Hope. With cellular phone, calculator and multipurpose tool firmly attached to his belt, Eric wove his way through a maze of lawyers, permits, electrical installations, heavy equipment rentals and tons of construction materials.

Just when Eric, Renato and company needed to make crucial decisions about the land, Todd Stong called. A retired officer in the Army Corps of Engineers with experience in Vietnam and Africa, Todd was interested in what he had seen of Common Hope on the Internet. It was a good thing Todd had a Ph.D. in soil mechanics because New Hope sat on the hardest, most difficult type of soil in Guatemala. For two weeks in September, 2000, Todd suggested where to put roads and lots, storm drainage pipes, a sewage treatment plant and strategic retaining walls. Todd calculated the precise angle that the entire property needed to slope in order to drain off any amount of water that a heavy rain, even a hurricane, might drop in the future. Finally, he outlined various methods to handle sewage.

Greg Scherer, chairman of the board of Common Hope, sensed a bigger challenge and stepped up to the plate. Greg, a recently retired executive and sponsor of several Common Hope children, had already made 12 trips to Guatemala. He was eager to get out of his corporate offices in Minneapolis and explore the terrain in Guatemala in depth and for a longer period of time. However, before he put on his jeans, he turned on his computer to research studies of wastewater treatment. The resource that helped him most was Biomass Project Nicaragua.[37]

Armed with the latest research, hours of conversation with engineers and 300 pages of notes, Greg oversaw the design of a state-of-the-art "wetland system." It would convert sewage into fertilizer, fodder and environmentally safe water run-off. This design moves waste through a series of concrete tanks and subsurface ponds. Plants growing in the ponds shelter bacteria that in turn convert pathogenic organisms into harmless organic matter. The facility requires little maintenance, produces no mosquitoes or odor and costs substantially less than other sewage treatment methods. In time, a committee of New Hope townspeople will maintain the system. Maybe Greg's sewage system won't become a national tourist attraction, but it is destined to interest anyone searching for replicable models of sustainable technology, especially for developing countries.

In the spring of 2001 Eric left his responsibilities in the hands of Jeff Barnes and Guatemalan Don Chepe. Jeff, from St. Louis, MO, with a post-graduate degree in economics and international affairs, left his career to build houses in Honduras after Hurricane Mitch. On a short vacation in Antigua, thinking of how he would market the cappuccino he was sipping, Jeff ran into someone who told him about Common Hope. Jeff's background was a match for the construction occurring at New Hope. By early 2001 he'd moved onsite next to Renato and family.

Don Chepe had just completed eight years in Antigua, supervising the construction of the Family Development Center. He brought with him to New Hope 20 of his best workers to teach construction skills to over 70 local Guatemalans. His stonemasons and carpenters had become highly skilled, bringing honor to themselves and their communities. Within sixteen months they completed New Hope's security and retaining walls, a two-story facility for warehouse and workshops and the first level of a multipurpose building to house a clinic, offices and volunteer workteams. These buildings are located at the project entrance and are referred to as the "service center."

Just down the main road is the village of New Hope. It is important in the design and philosophy of the organizers to keep "service center" and "village" as distinct areas—the former belonging to Common Hope as office space and workteam area and the latter belonging to the residents. A walk towards New Hope Village curves between the temporary school (that also serves as a community center) and a growing number of concrete-block houses, many of which belong to families made homeless by Hurricane Mitch.

Renato had been the one to focus on selecting families and building a community. He began in Guatemala City walking through the neighborhoods built on the sides of ravines damaged by the hurricane. Accompanied by the parish social worker, he met and talked with family after family. After listening to them tell how they survived the terror of poverty made worse by the hurricane, Renato explained Common Hope's vision of an entirely new community, where the residents would own their homes and land, and all the

children could go to school. In addition, Renato organized informational meetings held in a local church and invited those he met to come hear about New Hope. Almost 400 people attended these meetings, and of those approximately half indicated an interest in applying to be the first residents. This was a big step for families who had never even dreamed of moving out of the hillside slums and into their own homes, much less into a village that did not exist yet.

Social workers and a psychologist from the Antigua site joined Renato's team to develop an interview process. With 40 families waiting for interviews, it

Renato Westby, Director of Heart of Hope, takes a pickup load of supplies out to New Hope Village.

was imperative that they design exercises and interviews that would clearly communicate needed information between both parties.

Families were interviewed two at a time in separate interview rooms. Each family was interviewed as a whole, then separated into various groupings for additional discussions: parents together, each parent separately, and the children together. Gathered together, the family might say that there were no family problems, but alone or in a smaller group the mother, for example, might admit that the father had a drinking problem.

Each family participated in a problem-solving game, which demonstrated its ability to work together as a unit. In addition, two families were paired to solve a problem as a team, and their capacity to solve problems with strangers was also observed. From these exercises the interviewers learned a great deal about the families' strengths and weaknesses, including how they handled decision-making.

After the first round of interviews, 20 families were invited to continue into the second round, a series of workshops about conflict resolution and community formation. Observing families in these activities, Renato and his team discovered individuals who demonstrated maturity, stability, and the potential for community leadership. No one was allowed to see the land until the time had come to make a final commitment. The land at the time was being leveled for homes and roads and was not a pretty sight.

The nine families who formed the initial group of settlers at New Hope Village were taken to visit the land being developed. What brave spirits to look around at a few bare hills and to imagine living there! Undaunted, they worked together in the first construction of their own homes. These families would be the ones to set the tone for the entire community in the years to come. It was important, not that they be perfect, but that they have the potential to begin developing a community that would work together, solve its own internal conflicts, and make good decisions about its future.

The second group who moved to New Hope was made up of 18 families. Renato organized them into three groups to construct their houses, which, after completion, were assigned to families by lottery. When they had finished the construction, the families did not want to move in until their houses were blessed. Since they had all come from the same neighborhood, the priest from their church came out to do the blessings. The parents and children decorated their homes with brightly colored plastic banners and streamers. After the blessings, several fathers made short speeches, expressing what it meant to them to be moving into their own homes. One said, "Finally my children can all go to school, and I won't have to worry about their safety every time they walk out the door." Family members and New Hope volunteers shed many tears by the time all the houses were blessed and the newest group of families was ready to move into their new homes.

Each house in New Hope uses a gas stove and has a bathroom. The basic house plans have four rooms or approximately 500 square feet. Some families initially can afford to build only a two-room house, but they can add additional space later. The larger house occupies about 40% of a 1,250 square foot lot. When families are ready to move in, they sign a simple contract. They commit to make payments of about $30 per month for eight years on the no-interest loan of approximately $2,500 from Habitat for the four-room house. For five years all adults (over 14 years old and not in school) commit to contribute four hours a week (200 hours a year) in community service. They attend monthly workshops on community issues and may request sponsorship for their children if they desire. When the mortgage is paid and their community service requirements have been

The family of Oscar and Eliberta Díaz Villalobos, at the house they helped construct. They were one of the first families to move into New Hope Village.

met, the family receives title to their house and land.

A special grant to Common Hope made it possible for a psychologist to live in New Hope Village during 2002. He assisted in developing effective ways to build community and resolve conflicts.

Eliberta and Oscar Díaz Villalobos and their seven children were part of the "pioneer settlers" in New Hope village. Their family was the largest and the poorest of the first group. Even though Oscar had a job as a security guard in Guatemala City, he didn't always earn enough money to provide food for the family. Before they left the ravines and came to New Hope, Eliberta and Oscar had little hope of ever improving their situation. Eliberta said, "We came here to find a better, safer life for ourselves and our children." Their strict adherence to timely payments on their mortgage and other bills, in spite of their financial hardships, proved exemplary for all the other families. Also, by being willing to deal openly with their own problems in the community's group meetings, they set a high standard for honesty. Eliberta and Oscar's dreams for their children's education and for a safe community are coming true. At the same time, they are being personally challenged by their neighbors to learn and grow as individuals and as a family. Their situation illustrates how Common Hope expects families to take a look at themselves and make changes for a more wholesome community.

One day Greg Scherer, Jeff Barnes and I interrupted our walk around New Hope to rest in a shady spot between the two main fingers of land. After deciding that where we were sitting would be a good location for a compost pile, our conversation turned to the future of New Hope. "The future is right there," said Greg, pointing to the temporary school buildings. "The education of the children will change the nature of this place in a few generations. We won't be giving them the kind of rote system so prevalent in Guatemala. Our education will come from teachers who will help them learn to think."

We caught sight of Patty Zamora, Director of Education, standing across the road from the school. The past year had not been easy for her. Three

These temporary school buildings will be replaced by a permanent school as funds become available.

of her teachers had left because of New Hope's remote location. It took some of the teachers two hours and three bus rides to get home in the afternoon, leaving little or no time for teacher training.

I walked with Patty up the hill towards her office and asked, "How are you going to find new teachers and train them?"

"We'll find a way," she said. "We have so many children signed up for next year. The teachers will be there, and I will train them."

Such determination to bring quality education to Guatemalan children demonstrates the spirit of Common Hope—a spirit that builds futures on solid ground.

Common Hope has made a commitment to walk with the residents of New Hope Village, to train teachers and to provide health care and other basic services. However, Renato figures that both Habitat for Humanity and Common Hope will terminate their construction roles at New Hope Village in about 2010. By then, most of the 130 to 150 families who will eventually compose the town will own their own property. After all, the basic purpose of New Hope Village is to teach very poor Guatemalans how to take responsibility as landowners and to develop sufficient experience in managing their own town.

Children in New Hope's school learn analytical and critical thinking skills, a rarity in Guatemala.

Common Hope brings a great deal of energy to the challenge of developing self-determination within families. Woven into New Hope is a sense of self-worth and community—blessings enjoyed by children, parents, teachers, staff persons, workteams and long-term volunteers. After all, who needs hope most—poor Guatemalan families or foreign development workers? It's hard to say.

Common Hope for a New Millennium

Common Hope's fifteenth anniversary in November 2000 contained all things sweet and bitter that historical transitions are famous for. My wife, Sally, coordinated the planning, beginning many months earlier. The celebration brought to the Family Development Center in Antigua more than 100 sponsors and visitors from the U. S. and over 5,000 affiliated family members. The families did not come all at once, but were organized by villages to come on specific days. Every day for five consecutive days, as many as 1,500 people enjoyed piñatas, marimbas, weavings and healthful hot lunches coordinated by Ana and her kitchen staff. Kitty presented awards to outstanding students. Pat recognized children and their families who had worked hard to accomplish important goals. Bina Huebsch listened attentively as Dave Huebsch, the project's Founder and her husband of five years, congratulated the staff, volunteers and families for work well done. John presented to foreman Don Chepe and the construction workers a brass plaque engraved with all their names, an historical marker to be permanently mounted on the wall by the main entrance.

Tamalyn Jackson, Antigua Site Director, became Tamalyn Gutierrez after her marriage to Felipe Guttierez in 2002.

Perhaps the most visible symbol that the project had reached a milestone was the presence of 24-year-old Tamalyn Jackson, Antigua Site Director—a position she had accepted just two months before the celebration. In the summer of 2000 John's announcement of her appointment was greeted with heartfelt applause by staff and volunteers. Tamalyn, having grown up in Antigua, brought to the job a thorough knowledge of Guatemalan customs and language. She had already served as Director of Hospitality, a position that had put her in touch with every facet of

107

the project, from the U. S. office to the management team in Guatemala. Tamalyn interpreted Common Hope's determination to assist children's education and to empower families and communities as the desire to increase an individual's sense of choice. That thought shaped her dreams for the project as she looked out over thousands of people streaming through its doors.

The anniversary celebration carried the organization into a time of transition. In March of 2001 The Godchild Project became Common Hope, a name change timed to coincide with the opening of its new website—**www.commonhope.org**. Within a year construction workers would set their last concrete blocks at the Family Development Center and go on to jobs at New Hope or elsewhere. Kitty moved with Jessie into a private home that she built in Santa Ana, vacating the directorship of the education department in order to develop a teacher-training program on a national level. Two Guatemalans were employed as departmental directors—César Moreno in education and Gustavo Estrada in the clinic.

Tamalyn described what the moment was like from her perspective: "In previous years we needed warriors, creators and entrepreneurs. Now we need managers, nurturers and healers. We are moving into a 'proving ourselves time.'" Thus, her number one priority in the beginning of 2001 was to work with managers to clarify the project's goals and to improve communication skills. "My job is to help managers function as a team. Leaders who feel nurtured are more likely to nurture those under them," she said.

Committed to *Leadership That Builds People*[38], the title of a book she had translated into Spanish, Tamalyn worked with department heads and a psychologist to lead a series of in-service training events called "integration."[39] (See pages 91-93.) The objectives of integration were to develop critical thinking skills, to learn to communicate directly and to solve problems creatively. These skills would enable staff "to *want* to take responsibility for making choices, to *want* to be free and to *want* to hope for a better future for themselves and their families," said Tamalyn. Such goals were in line with Tamalyn's basic philosophy of increasing a sense of choice. But the integration workshops as well as the daily functioning of the project to which the staff and volunteers had become accustomed were interrupted by a series of events that no one could have predicted.

In the U. S. the millennium opened with an economic downturn. On September 11, 2001, terrorist attacks in the U. S. caused financial and political turmoil to reverberate around the world. Guatemalans found themselves under a regime that was compiling a record amount of corruption.[40] From airports to projects like Common Hope, these ominous intrusions demanded heightened security, better systems of financial accountability and tighter budgets. John, Tamalyn, Renato and their colleagues saw the handwriting on the wall and began to make new arrangements in priorities and programs.

Tamalyn made cuts in personnel, programs and expenditures. At New Hope Renato reduced the number of construction workers by half. The circumstances forced John to spend much more of his time fundraising in the U. S. His most difficult decision was to cut the project's most recent initiative, its national teacher education program. Regrettably, this move ended almost ten years of Kitty's involvement with the project.

Other significant departures, though not directly related to economic factors, marked the project's transition. Having tended to thousands of patients for more than a decade with Common Hope, Rosa Elena Solís left towards the end of 2002 for an excellent career opportunity elsewhere. A few months later, Adolfo Monroy, the project's first employee and recently married, moved on to new work and to raising a family.

During the economic downturn John's role gradually changed from managing construction and organization in Guatemala to a more concentrated fundraising schedule in the U. S. Financial leadership and a reorganization of the home office greatly facilitated this urgent focus. Wendy Cox, Development Director, began organizing fundraising full time. Sue Wheeler, with years in corporate management and an enlightening moment as translator for a Common Hope surgical team, became U.S. Director at the St. Paul office by mid-2002.

John's role in relation to the U. S. office and to the Guatemalan projects gradually grew into that of a manager of the directors of these operations. In this latter capacity, he could draw on years of experience to advise Sue, Tamalyn, Renato and the directors of possible additional projects. Such satellite projects would draw on the best elements of both the Antigua project and New Hope Village. In addition, John was increasingly being approached to advise other organizations interested in duplicating the model of Common Hope in Guatemala, Bolivia, Peru, Haiti and Africa. Although the global recession was making it more difficult to raise funds, the consequences mostly affected the poor, "All the more reason to be here," said John.

Common Hope carries into the new millennium a built-in creative tension. The tension arises from attending to two things at once—community development (New Hope Village) and family development (Antigua site). Most non-governmental organizations (NGOs) tend to drift in the direction of service to families only, a purely social welfare model. Few organizations attempt to improve entire communities by cultivating the needed "social capital"—neighborhood networks, grassroots leadership, organizational development skills, to name a few.[41] For certain, assembling an entire village from scratch at New Hope will sharpen skills in community building. The fact is, however, that the "drift" even at the Antigua site has been for years to strengthen cooperation with existing governmental agencies and community networks.

John believes that providing services to families and bringing resources to communities go hand in hand. The results are mutually beneficial and can best

At the first meeting of sponsor Mary Kay Rehmann and her godchild Julio Chiquitó there is an instant connection. The joy is in their faces.

be seen in the long-term effects. As an example he brings us back to where the book began, the story of Edi Rodríguez. John explains:

We expect that the children we sponsor, like Edi who returned to help his people, will bring improvement to their families and communities that we never dreamed of. In addition to education, health care, family empowerment and housing, we also want to build healthy communities.

Dave takes time out from his photography business in Minnesota to support these efforts. On occasions he and Bina travel to visit the work that he and his Huebsch family started almost two decades ago. He is happy to see that just as poor families are becoming more self-reliant, so the project is growing more independent. "Now it has a life of its own," he says.

The plans that Common Hope uses in the future will never come from a pre-packaged ideal imposed on the poor. Rather, as in a weaving, its design emerges from a variety of threads and colors. More specifically, Common Hope is being woven in large part from the ongoing interaction of volunteers and staff with Guatemalan families.

Much of Common Hope's work relies on volunteers' skills in health and human services, education, organizational development, technology and construction. Volunteers arrive mainly from the U. S. but also from many countries in the Americas, Caribbean, England, Europe and Africa. They range in age from late teens to retirees and even couples with small children. The annual number of short-term volunteers (who work from a few days to less than a year) is in the hundreds while approximately ten new long-term volunteers arrive each year to work with Common Hope. Most have studied beyond college and

Volunteers and staff show off their face paintings after a children's birthday party. Clockwise from bottom left: John Huebsch, Sara Ryan, Sally Thomas, Mary Thurmes, Pat Campbell, Zach Thomas, Kay Lantsberger, and Marcelo Pereira, son of volunteers.

stay a little more than two years on average. A few have never left. Only one in ten is fluent in Spanish upon arrival. Others usually need at least a year to feel that they can handle Spanish proficiently.[42] Some never do. Volunteers choose to live in a variety of arrangements—with families in the villages, in volunteer quarters on the project site, in rented apartments or in their own homes. At New Hope some volunteers live in houses among the villagers. So choices exist for those who prefer a rougher, more isolated experience (New Hope outside Guatemala City) or a setting that contains familiar amenities of North American culture (Antigua). Stipends are offered to encourage living in town or with Guatemalan families if a volunteer so desires. Those whose inquiries come from the integrity of their personal journey are more likely to be accepted than those who think their expertise is going to save the project or the poor.[43]

The continual influx of new volunteers brings new energies to the scene, but the Guatemalan staff will always be responsible for the main load of Common Hope's work. Most of the approximately 100 staff persons at the Antigua site grew up in the area. They are computer technicians, accountants, secretaries, social workers, educators, health professionals, sustainable technology specialists and more. A core group has worked there from the beginning. A number of staff members are previously sponsored children who were hired after graduation.

New employees and volunteers receive several weeks of orientation and then ongoing training in their jobs as needed. The project pays much of the cost of continuing education for Guatemalan employees who choose to further their careers in that manner.

Social workers Jaime Guerra Itzol and Sharon Dohse confer with María Eulalia Olayo about her new microbusiness. Her children Luky and Andi listen in.

When volunteers and staff weave their lives with Guatemalan families, the results are often unpredictable, yet always rich with valuable insights. Their letters and comments tell what they will remember for life.

- **Carrie Evans, volunteer from Colorado**: Working at Common Hope gave me hope about hands working together to find solutions. With local solutions comes a healthy local community that can effect change on a larger level. A healthy bright child with a solid education could develop a life in which peace and social justice become a career focus. I feel good about that. ¡Adelante!
- **Juan José, sponsored child, age 9**: The project gave a ball to my cousin. Now we play in the court at my village with my sisters. In our new house I don't worry when it rains.
- **Floridalma Castellano de García, staff social worker**: Building a house is not just hammering nails. It takes all my years in social work to help a family with a new house.
- **Mary Thurmes, volunteer from Minnesota**: My experience in Guatemala is now infused in every situation, job and relationship I have. I hope I am a more sincere, simple person. I need fewer clothes, less stuff and a house that has no more rooms than I need to live because I understand how precious land is.
- **Carmen, sponsored child, age 14**: I am grateful to the project because they helped us get electric lights to our village. Now I can read to my brothers and sisters.
- **Lorenzo Sipac, staff educator**: I'm glad I can help others like I have been helped. It's a different kind of education I'm receiving now.
- **Alden DeSoto, volunteer from California**: I had to come to terms with the absurd wealth and wastefulness of our society in the U. S. when I came back. The oppression I witnessed in Guatemala made me more aware of the inequities in my own country. I understand now that I'll never really be very satisfied if all I do is focus on my own life. I appreciate much more the importance of service.

- **María, sponsored child, age 11**: Thank you for the shoes for my birthday. My whole family thanks you for the hope and support you've given us.
- **Adolfo Monroy, staff legal advisor**: Working at Common Hope I've learned a lot about my culture. Knowing its problems, I can help families avoid making the same mistakes over and over.
- **Tom Lehmkuhl, workteam member from Minnesota**: My highlight was being hugged to death by little five-year-old Thelma when we were leaving. She was the youngest child of the family we built the house for. I still get emotional thinking about her.
- **Pilar Lima, mother of sponsored child**: My son and I were sick. The doctor examined us and gave us really good medicine. We are getting better. I received school supplies for my son. Thanks to all who have helped us. You are good people with a good heart. May God bless you. I am the mother of four kids and live alone without their father.
- **Edi Rodríguez, former sponsored child and now Guatemalan doctor**: I'm always amazed and grateful at how healing occurs. I want others to have the same excitement. It gives them hope, what the project gave me.
- **Gina Kossler, volunteer from California**: Volunteering helped me take money out of the picture to experience the true value of work. Since I left the project all my jobs have been bilingual positions that give me fond memories of Guatemala.
- **Ernesto, sponsored child, age 7**: If I could give thanks for all that the project has done for me and my little sisters…, but I don't have the words to say it.
- **Rosa Elena Solís, staff doctor**: I know my people, and they suffer more than they show. It will take a long time for things to change, but we are taking steps together day by day.
- **Gerry Carlsen, volunteer from California**: In Guatemala I think there is a softer, gentler way to be strong and that it's possible to be very happy with much less. Maybe this is what I'm learning."

In Common Hope, supporters, volunteers, staff and families participate in a process that benefits all parties. For the "gringos," it is often a reformation of priorities that helps them find a more wholesome path back home in a society stressed by the pressures of materialism. The Guatemalans benefit in a variety of practical ways, but most of all from being treated with dignity as human beings, a huge relief from the negative self-image that poverty breeds. Thus, two cultures find that in joining hands they are giving hope where each needs it the most. One can only conclude that this larger helping process is weaving *common* hope.

Jorge, Jennifer, Cristian and Brandon greet their sponsor family with excitement and hope in their eyes.

Zach Thomas

Afterword by John Huebsch
Executive Director of Common Hope

Common Hope's Executive Director, John Huebsch, reviews the progress on construction at New Hope Village.

Throughout Common Hope's history, I have been continually amazed at how the right people have showed up at the right time. Zach and Sally Thomas are such people. In these pages, Zach gracefully leads us through the complex journey of Common Hope's birth and childhood.

It has been my privilege to be a witness. I remember when Common Hope was nothing but an idea bouncing across my family's kitchen table. The reason our idea moved off the table is because we were willing to suspend our fear and make the irrational decision to step forward without knowing where it would lead. Our decision wasn't to start the dynamic project that exists today. It was to take the first step. I have witnessed that stepping out in faith is accompanied by a kind of grace that looks a lot like stumbling in all the right directions. I have come to implicitly trust this grace, which feels far less logical and more serendipitous than it might appear in retrospect.

This book gives readers a good taste of what has been our steady diet. Each of us has the power to make a profound difference in someone's life. And together, our power can change the world. That is the beauty of Common Hope. We are a group of ordinary people who have decided to live a different way, and together we are accomplishing the extraordinary. I have seen order emerge from chaos and hope arise from the deep conflict and struggle inherent in poverty.

Our story does not end with the last chapter. It continues to unfold every day with the same power as always. While many of the people you meet in these pages have moved on to other things, Ana, Renato, Tamalyn, Jeff and I, with many wonderful new people, wake up each day to chart our way through the maze of new challenges.

We have done well in weathering the downturn in the economy. In fact, we have responded creatively, using this time to reorganize ourselves and re-evaluate our goals and priorities. At New Hope, the water, sewage and electrical systems are installed; our temporary school educates 148 primary students; we are designing our permanent school, which should serve about 650 students; and 30 more families will move into New Hope village within the next months. In Antigua, 2,566 students are starting the 2003 school year; a house is built each week; patients stream into the clinic; our surgical team is operating today in a nearby village; and the Guatemalan staff is taking a larger leadership role in guiding our work. Our U. S. office continues to play a major role in supporting the work in Guatemala.

Soon we will be reaching out to even more impoverished people as we prepare to establish another project site in Guatemala. As long as there is poverty, we have work to do.

While I am proud of what we have accomplished, I am also humbled. The reality of the project has far surpassed our dreams—it has become more than we ever imagined possible. This is due to the courageous vision of my parents, the generosity of our donors, the hard work of our staff, and the grace of God. It is my hope is that we never become so comfortable with our success that we forget to live on the edge with the poor and remember that it is they whom we serve, and it is they who teach us so much.

I am excited to see where this journey leads us.

John Huebsch
Antigua, Guatemala
February 10, 2003

Notes

Letting Go and Dreaming

[1] In addition to the 28,000 who died, the earthquake left 70,000 wounded and 1,800,000 without homes. Avendaño, Nancy, "Disastre nacional," *Domingo: Revista semanal de Prensa Libre.* Número 1028: 4 de febrero de 2001, p. 4.

[2] In 1986 the Huebsches began using "The Godchild Project" as the title by which their organization would be known in English. In 1991 an organization with a similar name, doing similar work, moved to Antigua. To avoid confusion and to reflect having grown larger than a child sponsorship program, The Godchild Project changed its name to Common Hope in March of 2001.

Common Hope has had two different Spanish names. In the early 1990s it used the name *Proyecto Niños de Dios* (Children of God Project). Upon learning that another organization had a similar name, the project in 1994 changed the Spanish name to *Familias de Esperanza* (Families of Hope). The second project site begun in 1999 near Guatemala City is called *Nueva Esperanza* (New Hope). Common Hope is also incorporated in Guatemala as a nonprofit foundation with the title *Fundación de Familias de Esperanza* (Foundation of Families of Hope).

[3] Peat, F. David, *Synchronicity: The Bridge Between Matter and Mind.* New York: Bantam Books, 1987.

[4] See Huebsch, Bill, *A Spirituality of Wholeness: A New Look at Grace.* Mystic, CT: Twenty Third Publications, 1988.

Ties That Bind

[5] See the booklet written in 2000 by the mission's head cook, Encarnación Ajcot as told to Myra Maldonado, *Maltiox Tat, "Thank*

You Father": A History of Father Gregory Schaffer and the San Lucas Tolimán Mission. La Parroquia, San Lucas Tolimán, Dept. Sololá 07013, Guatemala, C.A. or San Lucas Mission Office, 1400 6th Street North, New Ulm, MN 56073-2099.

Also, see the article by Randolph-Macon Woman's College Economics Professor John Abell, "Peace in Guatemala? The Story of San Lucas Tolimán" in Brauer, Jurgen and Gissy, William, *Economics of Conflict and Peace.* Aldershot, England: Avebury, 1997.

[6] Perera, Victor, *Unfinished Conquest: The Guatemala Tragedy.* Berkeley, CA: University of California Press, 1993, p. 182. "In 1987, the municipality's records listed gunshot wounds as the third highest cause of death in Atitlán, behind infant diarrhea and respiratory diseases." (p. 171)

[7] Bogart, Rosemary, *St. Cloud Visitor.* June 18, 1987, p. 22.

[8] Ardón, Patricia, *Post-war Reconstruction in Central America.* Great Britain:
Oxfam, 1999, p. 27. The Esquipulas II Accords were signed in August, 1987.

[9] Perera, ibid. p. 289.

[10] Martín-Baró, Ignacio, *Writings for a Liberation Psychology.* Cambridge, MA: Harvard University Press, 1994, p. 91. The author was one of 6 priests assassinated in El Salvador, Nov. 16, 1989. See also Freire, Paulo, *Pedagogy of the Oppressed.* New York, NY: The Continuum Publishing Company, 1999.

Father-Son Team

[11] Statistics are derived from Common Hope's social work department representing the population served in fourteen villages south and east

of Antigua.   Communication from Pat Campbell, Director of Department of Social Work, November, 2001.

[12] Barry, Tom, *Inside Guatemala.* Alburquerque, NM: The Inter-Hemispheric Education Resource Center, 1992, p. 169, 175.

[13] North, Douglass, C., *Institutions, Institutional Change and Economic Performance.* Cambridge, UK: Cambridge University Press, 1990, p.114. "Every detail of the economy as well as the polity [in Central America] was structured with the objective of furthering the interests of the [Spanish] crown in the creation of the most powerful empire since Rome." (p. 114)
"U.S. economic history has been characterized by a federal political system, checks and balances, and a basic structure of property rights...essential to the creation of capital markets and economic growth.   ...Latin American economic history, in contrast, has perpetuated the centralized, bureaucratic traditions carried over from its Spanish/Portuguese heritage.   ...In the latter, personalistic relationships are still the key to much of the political and economic exchange." (p. 116-117)

[14] Perera, ibid., pp. 1-9.

[15] Abell, John D., "Economic Theory and Reality: Evidence from San Lucas Tolimán and the Rest of the World." Paper delivered at Latin American Studies Association: Washington, DC, September 6-8, 2001, p. 12-13.

[16] Kinsler, Ross and Gloria Kinsler, *The Biblical Jubilee and the Struggle for Life.* New York: Orbis Books, Maryknoll, 2000, p. 4.

We're All In This Together

[17] Common Hope's *Spring Newsletter, 1993.*

[18] Common Hope's *Christmas Newsletter*, 1994.

121

[19] Barry, ibid., p. 175 ff.

[20] As a group, women had significantly lower statistical rates than these averages. Notice that in this system it is possible to graduate from high school, to be considered qualified to teach and, thus, end up teaching students who are in fact only a few years younger than the teacher. In the last decade more options have been added such as careers in technical design, computer science, electronics, automotive mechanics and administration. For those who finish the sixth grade, vocational training options can be found now in carpentry, sewing classes, beautician schools and cooking classes. Some students choose to attend vocational training opportunities while continuing in junior high school. (Personal communication from Kitty Brown, November, 2001.)

[21] Comparing statistics in 1999 with 1991, 81% of 7- to 12-year-olds were enrolled in elementary school (up 30%), 21% of 13- to 15-year-olds in junior high school (up 6%), and 13% of 16- to 19-year-olds in senior high school (up 12%). In each category little more than half would be promoted to the next grade and 15% would quit. *Informe del Diagnóstico del Sector Educativo*, USAID/G-CAP, Guatemala: Management Systems International, March, 2001, Anexo 3, p. 2.

[22] The percentage of the Gross National Product that Guatemala spent for education in 1971 was 1.7% and in 1999 was 1.6%, lowest of all the Latin American countries. Avendaño, Nancy, "Déficit Educativo," *Prensa Libre: Guatemala.* 4 de noviembre de 2001, p. 8-11.

[23] Freire, ibid., p. 53 ff.

[24] Jeavons, John, *How to Grow More Vegetables.* Berkeley, CA: Ten Speed Press, 1995. This was the main resource for the gardening program and is also available in Spanish.

[25] Cácerez, Armando, *Plantas de Uso Medicinal en Guatemala.* Universidad de San Carlos de Guatemala, Centroamérica: Editorial Universitaria, 1996.

[26] For more information on Larry Winiarski's research on stoves, consult the Internet website, "Aprovecho Research Center."

Curing and Caring

[27] Website, *Statistics in Latin America – LANIC,* "Pan American Health Organization – Health in the Americas, Guatemala," 1998 edition, p. 2.

[28] Ibid.

[29] Dubrke, Karen and D. Smith. *Guatemala in Context.* CEDEPCA: Guatemala City, 15th Edition, Feb., 2000, p. 8: "According to UN standards, those who earn less than US$1 per day live in extreme poverty. 53.3% of Guatemalans fall into this category."

[30] Ibid.

[31] Center for International Health Information (CIHI). See website for USAid.gov/countries/gt/gt.txt, 1996.

[32] *Prensa Libre,* "Resumen Annual 2001," 28 de diciembre de 2001, p. 12.

[33] *Prensa Libre,* February, 1998.

[34] In 1993 Kitty began adapting ideas used for years with poor women in African villages. Her main resource was the book by Anne Hope and Sally Timmel, *Training for Transformation: A Handbook for Community Workers,* Books 1,2,3. Zimbabwe: Mambo Press, Gweru, 1984 (edition 1988). Book 4, Southampton Row, London: Intermediate Technology Publications Ltd., 1999.

[35] Covey, Stephen R., *Principle-Centered Leadership*, Simon & Schuster, 1992.

[36] Processes cultivating integration are based on the research and theory of the Salvadoran, Ignacio Martín-Baró, and the Brazilian, Paulo Freire. See footnote 10.

Hope From a Hurricane

[37] See the website "Biomass Project Nicaragua" or "Wetland System in Nicaragua."

Common Hope for a New Millennium

[38] Richards, James B., *Leadership That Builds People.* Huntsville, AL: Impact Ministries, Vol. 1, 1993; Vol.2, 1997.

[39] The theory of integration (*concientización*) comes from the research of Ignacio Martín-Baró and Paulo Freire and their theories of development work. See footnote 10.

[40] *Prensa Libra*, "Campante, la corrupción avanza." Guatemala, domingo 6 de enero de 2002. "Este ha sido el gobierno del que más se ha sabido sobre corrupción." (p. 14) "Openly, the corruption advances: This has been the government about which more is known regarding corruption." (Author's translation)

[41] Abom, William, "Social Capital, Social Organising, Non-governmental Organisations and Development: A Guatemalan Case Study." Thesis submitted by William Abom to the Development Studies Centre, Kimmage Manor, Dublin, in partial fulfillment of the requirements for the MA in Development Studies, 2001.

[42] Author's note: Volunteers who learn Spanish more quickly tend to be younger and to do work that demands a high level of interaction with the Spanish-speaking population.

[43] From data gathered by questionnaires and interviews. Author, November, 2001.

About the Author

Zach Thomas, a former Presbyterian minister and hospital chaplain, studied health traditions in China, Thailand, Greece, Turkey and Central America. He wrote *Healing Touch: The Church's Forgotten Language* (Louisville, KY: Westminster/John Knox Press, 1994). For five years beginning in 1997 he and his wife, Sally, worked as volunteers with Common Hope serving poor families near Antigua, Guatemala. Zach coordinated a gardening/medicinal herb program and wrote stories for Guatemalan children. (The series is now available in English and Spanish at 1stBooks.com.). In Charlotte Zach works with Latino jail inmates, and Sally operates historic walking tours. Their daughter, Leigh, and her husband, Cory Jones, live nearby and have one son, Zacory Grayson Jones.

About the Illustrator

Mynor Alvarado was in high school when he came to the Common Hope's clinic because of tingling in his fingers. The doctors, one of whom was visiting on a workteam, discovered a tumor growing in Mynor's shoulder. Arrangements were made for Mynor to be operated on in Minnesota. After nine hours of surgery the tumor was successfully removed and fortunately was benign. Donating their services were the airlines, the medical center and the thoracic surgeon who happened to be a native Guatemalan.

Mynor is still gaining better use of his fingers as he pursues his dream of becoming an architect. Drawing the illustrations was his way of showing gratitude to the project for saving his life.

Gifts and Support

Common Hope
550 Vandalia Street
P.O. Box 14298
St. Paul, MN 55114

Phone: 651-917-0917
Fax: 651-917-7458
E-mail: info@mn.commonhope.org
Website: www.commonhope.org

Field Address

Familias de Esperanza
KM 2, Carretera a San Juan
Antigua, Sacatepequez 03901
Guatemala, Centro América

Phone/Fax: 011-502-832-4111
E-mail: info@guate.commonhope.org